The Complete Breville Smart Air Fryer Oven Cookbook for Beginners

250 Quick & Easy Air Fryer Oven Recipes for Healthy Meals

Jamie Johnson

CONTENTS

Fish & Seafood 74

Breakfast 80

INTRODUCTION

Hey AirFrying Lover! Welcome to Breville Smart Oven Air Fryer cookbook!

I hope you'll love this book as much as I loved to cook the recipes inside this fantastic AirFryer Oven appliance. If you're new to air frying or you are a seasoned air fryer cook, this book has probably the best recipes in my cooking experience, for great meals everyone will enjoy.

We all know that thee air fryer is a remarkable kitchen appliance. It lets you cook delicious food without using all that fat and oil. And now it joins forces with Breville Oven to create the ultimate Air Frying, Toaster, Oven experience. You'll be able to create yummy and healthy meals.

No matter what type of recipe you're looking for...I've got one for you. Appetizers, French fries, nuggets, wings, even desserts. Poultry, and meat options are also plentiful. I didn't forget about my fellow vegans and vegetarians for easy plant-based recipes that are sure to be delightful. When it comes to breakfast and dessert, I've got some healthy choices for you. And I have some recipes that are tasty and decadent, using ingredients that are sure to make your mouth water in anticipation.

Be warned – the recipes in this book aren't for those who are on a diet and watching their weigh. Though, it's possible to stick to a meal plan, with some careful preparation. Therefore the recipes presented here are to be savored and enjoyed. But even if you're watching what you eat, it all comes down to balancing your diet. Use this cookbook to create unforgettable cooking experience with friends, family or yourself. Why not something a little scrumptious?!

Let's jump into the recipes for some real time game!

APPETIZERS & SIDE DISHES

Cheddar Tortilla Chips

Prep + Cook Time: 55 minutes | Serves: 6

Ingredients

1 cup flour
Salt and black pepper to taste

1 tbsp golden flaxseed meal
2 cups shredded Cheddar cheese

Directions

Melt cheddar cheese in the microwave for 1 minute. Once melted, add the flour, salt, flaxseed meal, and pepper. Mix well with a fork.

On a board, place the dough, and knead it with hands while warm until the ingredients are well combined. Divide the dough into 2 and with a rolling pin, roll them out flat into 2 rectangles.

Use a pastry cutter, to cut out triangle-shaped pieces and line them in 1 layer on a baking dish. Grease the frying basket with cooking spray.

Arrange some triangle chips in 1 layer in the basket without touching or overlapping; spray them with cooking spray. Cook for 10 minutes on AirFry function. Serve with a cheese dip.

Mustard Cheddar Twists

Prep + Cook Time: 45 minutes | Serves: 8

INGREDIENTS

2 cups cauliflower florets, steamed
1 egg
3 ½ oz oats
1 red onion, diced

1 tsp mustard
5 oz cheddar cheese
Salt and black pepper to taste

DIRECTIONS

Preheat Breville on AirFry to 350 F, place the oats in a food processor, and pulse until they are the consistency of breadcrumbs. Place the steamed florets in a cheesecloth and squeeze out the excess liquid.

Place the cauliflower florets in a large bowl. Add the rest of the ingredients to the bowl. Mix well with hands to combine the ingredients completely. Take a little bit of the mixture and twist it into a straw.

Place on a lined baking tray and repeat with the rest of the mixture. Cook for 10 minutes, turn over and cook for an additional 10 minutes.

Garlicky Mushroom Spaghetti

Prep + Cook Time: 10 minutes | Serves: 4

INGREDIENTS

½ lb white button mushrooms, sliced
1 tsp butter
2 garlic cloves, chopped

12 oz spaghetti, cooked
14 oz mushroom sauce
Salt and black pepper to taste

DIRECTIONS

Preheat Breville on AirFry function to 400 F. In the Air Fryer basket, place the butter and garlic; cook for 3 minutes. Add in the mushrooms and cook for 5 more minutes. Remove to a pan over medium heat and stir in mushroom sauce. Season with salt and pepper and cook until heated, 1-2 minutes. Pour over cooked spaghetti and serve.

Pancetta & Goat Cheese Bombs with Almonds

Prep + Cook Time: 25 minutes | Serves: 10

Ingredients

16 oz soft goat cheese
2 tbsp fresh rosemary, finely chopped
1 cup almonds, chopped into small pieces

Salt and black pepper
15 dried plums, chopped
15 pancetta slices

Directions

Line the Breville Air Fryer basket with baking paper. In a bowl, add cheese, rosemary, almonds, salt, pepper and plums; stir well. Roll into balls and wrap with a pancetta slice. Arrange the bombs in the basket and cook for 10 minutes at 400 F. Check at the 5-minute mark, to avoid overcooking. When ready, let cool before removing them from the oven. Serve with toothpicks.

Ham & Mozzarella Eggplant Boats

Prep + Cook Time: 17 minutes | Serves: 2

INGREDIENTS

1 eggplant
4 ham slices, chopped
1 cup shredded mozzarella cheese, divided

1 tsp dried parsley
Salt and black pepper to taste

DIRECTIONS

Preheat Breville on AirFry function to 330 F, peel the eggplant and cut it lengthwise in half; scoop some of the flesh out. Season with salt and pepper. Divide half of mozzarella cheese between the eggplants and place the ham on top of the mozzarella. Top with the remaining mozzarella, sprinkle with parsley and cook for 12 minutes.

Paprika Pickle Chips

Prep + Cook Time: 20 minutes | Serves: 3

Ingredients

36 sweet pickle chips
1 cup buttermilk
3 tbsp smoked paprika

2 cups flour
¼ cup cornmeal
Salt and black pepper to taste

Directions

Preheat Breville on Air Fryer function to 400 F. In a bowl, mix flour, paprika, pepper, salt, cornmeal and powder. Place pickles in buttermilk and set aside for 5 minutes. Dip the pickles in the spice mixture and place them in the cooking basket. Cook for 10 minutes.

Mini Salmon & Cheese Quiches

Prep + Cook Time: 20 minutes | Serves: 15

Ingredients

15 mini tart cases
4 eggs, lightly beaten
½ cup heavy cream
Salt and black pepper

3 oz smoked salmon
6 oz cream cheese, divided into 15 pieces
6 fresh dill

Directions

Mix together eggs and cream in a pourable measuring container. Arrange the tarts into the basket. Pour in mixture into the tarts, about halfway up the side and top with a piece of salmon and a piece of cheese. Cook for 10 minutes at 340 F on Bake function, regularly check to avoid overcooking. Sprinkle with dill and serve chilled.

Pineapple Spareribs

Prep + Cook Time: 30 minutes | Serves: 4

Ingredients

2 lb cut spareribs
7 oz salad dressing
1 (5-oz) can pineapple juice

2 cups water
Garlic salt to taste
Salt and black pepper

Directions

Sprinkle the ribs with salt and pepper, and place them in a saucepan. Pour water and cook the ribs for 12 minutes on high heat. Drain the ribs and arrange them in the frying basket; sprinkle with garlic salt. Cook for 15 minutes at 390 F on AirFry function. Prepare the sauce by combining the salad dressing and the pineapple juice. Serve the ribs drizzled with the sauce.

Sweet Coconut Shrimp

Prep + Cook Time: 30 minutes | Serves: 5

Ingredients

1 lb jumbo shrimp, peeled and deveined
¾ cup shredded coconut
1 tbsp maple syrup

½ cup breadcrumbs
⅓ cup cornstarch
½ cup milk

Directions

Pour the cornstarch in a zipper bag, add shrimp, zip the bag up and shake vigorously to coat with the cornstarch. Mix the syrup and milk in a bowl and set aside. In a separate bowl, mix the breadcrumbs and shredded coconut. Open the zipper bag and remove each shrimp while shaking off excess starch.

Dip each shrimp in the milk mixture and then in the crumbs mixture while pressing loosely to trap enough crumbs and coconut. Place the coated shrimp in the basket without overcrowding. Cook for 12 minutes at 350 F on AirFry function, flipping once halfway through.

Cinnamon Mixed Nuts

Prep + Cook Time: 25 minutes | Serves: 5

Ingredients

½ cup pecans
½ cup walnuts
½ cup almonds
A pinch cayenne pepper

2 tbsp sugar
2 tbsp egg whites
2 tsp cinnamon

Directions

Add the pepper, sugar, and cinnamon to a bowl and mix them well; set aside. In another bowl, mix in the pecans, walnuts, almonds, and egg whites. Add the spice mixture to the nuts and give it a good mix. Lightly grease the frying basket with cooking spray.

Pour in the nuts, and cook them for 10 minutes on AirFry function at 350 F. Stir the nuts using a wooden vessel, and cook for further for 10 minutes. Pour the nuts in the bowl. Let cool.

Apple & Cinnamon Chips

Prep + Cook Time: 25 minutes | Serves: 2

Ingredients

1 tsp sugar
1 tsp salt
1 whole apple, sliced

½ tsp cinnamon
Confectioners' sugar for serving

Directions

Preheat your Breville to 400 F. In a bowl, mix cinnamon, salt and sugar; add the apple slices. Place the prepared apple spices in the cooking basket and cook for 10 minutes on Bake function. Dust with sugar and serve.

Sesame Cabbage & Prawns Egg Roll Wraps

Prep + Cook Time: 50 minutes | Serves: 4

Ingredients

2 tbsp vegetable oil
1-inch piece fresh ginger, grated
1 tbsp minced garlic
1 carrot, cut into strips
¼ cup chicken broth
2 tbsp reduced-sodium soy sauce

1 tbsp sugar
1 cup shredded Napa cabbage
1 tbsp sesame oil
8 cooked prawns, minced
1 egg
8 egg roll wrappers

Directions

In a skillet over high heat, heat vegetable oil, and cook ginger and garlic for 40 seconds, until fragrant. Stir in carrot and cook for another 2 minutes. Pour in chicken broth, soy sauce, and sugar and bring to a boil.

Add cabbage and let simmer until softened, for 4 minutes. Remove skillet from the heat and stir in sesame oil. Let cool for 15 minutes. Strain cabbage mixture, and fold in minced prawns. Whisk an egg in a small bowl. Fill each egg roll wrapper with prawn mixture, arranging the mixture just below the center of the wrapper.

Fold the bottom part over the filling and tuck under. Fold in both sides and tightly roll up. Use the whisked egg to seal the wrapper. Place the rolls into a greased frying basket, spray with oil and cook for 12 minutes at 370 F on AirFry function, turning once halfway through.

Rosemary Potatoes

Prep + Cook Time: 35 minutes | Serves: 4

Ingredients

1.5 pounds potatoes, halved
2 tbsp olive oil
3 garlic cloves, grated

1 tbsp minced fresh rosemary
1 tsp salt
¼ tsp freshly ground black pepper

Directions

In a bowl, mix potatoes, olive oil, garlic, rosemary, salt, and pepper, until they are well-coated. Arrange the potatoes in the basket and cook t 360 F on AirFry function for 25 minutes, shaking twice during the cooking. Cook until crispy on the outside and tender on the inside.

Crunchy Mozzarella Sticks with Sweet Thai Sauce

Prep + Cook Time: 2 hrs 20 minutes | Serves: 4

Ingredients

12 mozzarella string cheese
2 cups breadcrumbs
3 eggs

1 cup sweet thai sauce
4 tbsp skimmed milk

Directions

Pour the crumbs in a bowl. Crack the eggs into another bowl and beat with the milk. One after the other, dip each cheese sticks in the egg mixture, in the crumbs, then egg mixture again and then in the crumbs again.

Place the coated cheese sticks on a cookie sheet and freeze for 1 to 2 hours. Preheat Breville on AirFry function to 380 F. Arrange the sticks in the frying basket without overcrowding. Cook for 8 minutes, flipping them halfway through cooking to brown evenly. Cook in batches. Serve with a sweet thai sauce.

Chili Cheese Crisps

Prep + Cook Time: 25 minutes | Serves: 3

Ingredients

4 tbsp grated cheese + extra for rolling
1 cup flour + extra for kneading
¼ tsp chili powder

½ tsp baking powder
3 tsp butter
A pinch of salt

Directions

In a bowl, mix in the cheese, flour, baking powder, chili powder, butter, and salt. The mixture should be crusty. Add some drops of water and mix well to get a dough. Remove the dough on a flat surface.

Rub some extra flour in your palms and on the surface, and knead the dough for a while. Using a rolling pin, roll the dough out into a thin sheet. With a pastry cutter, cut the dough into your desired lings' shape. Add the cheese lings to the basket, and cook for 8 minutes at 350 F on AirFry function, flipping once halfway through.

Chicken Wings in Alfredo Sauce

Prep + Cook Time: 60 minutes | Serves: 4

Ingredients

1 ½ pounds chicken wings, pat- dried
Salt to taste

½ cup Alfredo sauce

Directions

Preheat Breville on AirFry function to 370 F. Season the wings with salt. Arrange them in the fryer, without touching. Cook in batches if needed, for 20 minutes, until no longer pink in the center. Increase to 390 F and cook for 5 minutes more. Remove to a big bowl and coat well with the sauce. Serve.

Mustard Chicken Wings

Prep + Cook Time: 45 minutes | Serves: 8

Ingredients

½ tsp celery salt
½ tsp bay leaf powder
½ tsp ground black pepper
½ tsp paprika

¼ tsp dry mustard
¼ tsp cayenne pepper
¼ tsp allspice
2 pounds chicken wings

Directions

Grease the frying basket and preheat Breville to 340 F on AirFry function. In a bowl, mix celery salt, bay leaf powder, black pepper, paprika, dry mustard, cayenne pepper, and allspice. Coat the wings thoroughly in this mixture.

Arrange the wings in an even layer in the basket. Cook the chicken until it's no longer pink around the bone, for 30 minutes. Then, increase the temperature to 380 F and cook for 6 minutes more, until crispy on the outside.

Parmesan Chicken Nuggets

Prep + Cook Time: 25 minutes | Serves: 4

Ingredients

1 lb chicken breast, boneless, skinless, cubed
½ tsp ground black pepper
¼ tsp kosher salt
¼ tsp seasoned salt

2 tbsp olive oil
5 tbsp plain breadcrumbs
2 tbsp panko breadcrumbs
2 tbsp grated Parmesan cheese

Directions

Preheat Breville on AirFry function to 380 F and grease. Season the chicken with pepper, kosher salt, and seasoned salt; set aside. In a bowl, pour olive oil. In a separate bowl, add crumb, and Parmesan cheese.

Place the chicken pieces in the oil to coat, then dip into breadcrumb mixture, and transfer to the Air Fryer basket. Lightly spray chicken with cooking spray.

Cook the chicken for 10 minutes, flipping once halfway through. Cook until golden brown on the outside and no more pink on the inside.

Jalapeños Peppers with Chicken & Bacon

Prep + Cook Time: 40 minutes | Serves: 4

Ingredients

8 Jalapeno peppers, halved lengthwise
4 chicken breasts, butterflied and halved
6 oz cream cheese
6 oz Cheddar cheese

16 slices bacon
1 cup breadcrumbs
Salt and black pepper to taste
2 eggs

Directions

Season the chicken with pepper and salt on both sides. In a bowl, add cream cheese, cheddar, a pinch of pepper and salt. Mix well. Take each jalapeno and spoon in the cheese mixture to the brim. On a working board, flatten each piece of chicken and lay 2 bacon slices each on them. Place a stuffed jalapeno on each laid out chicken and bacon set, and wrap the jalapenos in them.

Preheat Breville on AirFry function to 350 F. Add the eggs to a bowl and pour the breadcrumbs in another bowl. Also, set a flat plate aside. Take each wrapped jalapeno and dip it into the eggs and then in the breadcrumbs. Place them on the flat plate. Lightly grease the fryer basket with cooking spray. Arrange 4-5 breaded jalapenos in the basket, and cook for 7 minutes.

Turn the jalapenos and cook for 4 minutes. Once ready, remove them onto a paper towel-lined plate. Serve with a sweet dip for an enhanced taste.

Homemade Chicken Thighs

Prep + Cook Time: 30 minutes | Serves: 4

Ingredients

1 pound chicken thighs
½ tsp salt

¼ tsp black pepper
¼ tsp garlic powder

Directions

Season the thighs with salt, pepper, and garlic powder. Arrange thighs, skin side down, on the Breville Air Fryer basket and cook until golden brown for 20 minutes at 350 F on Bake function.

BBQ Full Chicken

Prep + Cook Time: 25 minutes | Serves: 3

Ingredients

1 whole small chicken, cut into pieces
1 tsp salt
1 tsp smoked paprika

1 tsp garlic powder
1 cup BBQ sauce

Directions

Mix salt, paprika, and garlic and coat chicken pieces. Place them skin-side down in the toaster oven. Cook for around 15 minutes at 400 F on Bake function, until slightly golden. Remove to a plate and brush with barbecue sauce.

Return the chicken to the oven, skin-side up, and cook for 5 minutes at 340 F. Serve with more barbecue sauce.

Sesame Sticky Chicken Wings

Prep + Cook Time: 55 minutes | Serves: 4

Ingredients

1 pound chicken wings
1 cup soy sauce, divided
½ cup brown sugar
½ cup apple cider vinegar
2 tbsp fresh ginger, minced

2 tbsp fresh garlic, minced
1 tsp finely ground black pepper
2 tbsp cornstarch
2 tbsp cold water
1 tsp sesame seeds

Directions

In a bowl, add chicken wings, and pour in half cup soy sauce. Refrigerate for 20 minutes; drain and pat dry. Arrange the wings on the Air Fryer basket and cook for 30 minutes at 380 F on AirFry function, turning once halfway through. Make sure you check them towards the end to avoid overcooking.

In a skillet and over medium heat, stir sugar, half cup soy sauce, vinegar, ginger, garlic, and black pepper. Cook until sauce has reduced slightly, about 4 to 6 minutes.

Dissolve 2 tbsp of cornstarch in cold water, in a bowl, and stir in the slurry into the sauce, until it thickens, for 2 minutes. Pour the sauce over wings and sprinkle with sesame seeds.

Cheese & Rice Stuffed Mushrooms

Prep + Cook Time: 30 minutes | Serves: 10

Ingredients

10 Swiss brown mushrooms
Olive oil to brush the mushrooms
1 cup cooked brown rice

1 cup grated Grana Padano cheese
1 tsp dried mixed herbs
Salt and black pepper

Directions

Brush mushrooms with oil and arrange onto the Breville Air Fryer basket. In a bowl, mix rice, cheese, herbs, salt and pepper. Stuff the mushrooms with the mixture. Cook in the toaster oven for 14 minutes at 360 F on Bake function. Make sure the mushrooms cooked until golden and the cheese has melted. Serve with fresh herbs.

Parmesan Dill Pickles

Prep + Cook Time: 35 minutes | Serves: 4

Ingredients

3 cups Dill Pickles, sliced, drained
2 eggs
2 tsp water

1 cup Grated Parmesan cheese
1 ½ cups breadcrumbs, smooth
Black pepper to taste

Directions

Add the breadcrumbs and black pepper to a bowl and mix well; set aside. In another bowl, crack the eggs and beat with the water. Set aside. Add the cheese to a separate bowl; set aside.

Preheat Breville on AirFry function to 400 F.

Pull out the fryer basket and spray it lightly with cooking spray. Dredge the pickle slices it in the egg mixture, then in breadcrumbs and then in cheese. Place them in the fryer.

Slide the fryer basket back in and cook for 4 minutes. Turn them and cook for further for 5 minutes, until crispy. Serve with a cheese dip.

Garlicky Roasted Chicken with Lemon

Prep + Cook Time: 60 minutes | Serves: 4

Ingredients

1 chicken (around 3.5 lb), rinsed, pat-dried
1 tbsp olive oil
1 tsp salt

¼ tsp black pepper
1 lemon, cut into quarters
5 garlic cloves

Directions

Rub chicken with olive oil and season with salt and pepper. Stuff with lemon and garlic cloves into the cavity.

Arrange chicken, breast-side down, on the Breville Air Fryer basket. Tuck the legs and wings tips under. Cook for 45 minutes at 350 F on Bake function. Let rest for 5-6 minutes, then carve.

Savory Cod Fingers

Prep + Cook Time: 25 minutes | Serves: 3

Ingredients

2 cups flour
Salt and black pepper to taste
1 tsp seafood seasoning
2 whole eggs, beaten
1 cup cornmeal

1 pound cod fillets, cut into fingers
2 tbsp milk
2 eggs, beaten
1 cup breadcrumbs

Directions

Preheat Breville on Air Fryer function to 400 F. In a bowl, mix beaten eggs with milk. In a separate bowl, mix flour, cornmeal, and seafood seasoning. In another mixing bowl, mix spices with the eggs. In a third bowl, pour the breadcrumbs.

Dip cod fingers in the seasoned flour mixture, followed by a dip in the egg mixture and finally coat with breadcrumbs. Place the fingers in your Air Fryer basket and cook for 10 minutes.

Eggplant Cakes with Yogurt

Prep + Cook Time: 20 minutes | Serves: 4

INGREDIENTS

1 ½ cups flour
1 tsp cinnamon
3 eggs
2 tsp baking powder
2 tbsp sugar
1 cup milk

2 tbsp butter, melted
1 tbsp yogurt
½ cup shredded eggplant
Pinch of salt
2 tbsp cream cheese

DIRECTIONS

Preheat Breville on AirFry function to 350 F, and on a bowl, whisk the eggs along with the sugar, salt, cinnamon, cream cheese, flour, and baking powder. In another bowl, combine all of the liquid ingredients. Gently combine the dry and liquid mixtures; stir in eggplant.

Line the muffin tins and pour the batter inside; cook for 12 minutes. Check with a toothpick: you may need to cook them for an additional 2 to 3 minutes.

Weekend Chicken Wings

Prep + Cook Time: 20 minutes | Serves: 3

Ingredients

15 chicken wings
Salt and black pepper to taste
⅓ cup chili sauce

⅓ cup butter
½ tbsp vinegar

Directions

Preheat Breville on AirFry function to 360 F. Season the wings with pepper and salt. Add them to the toaster oven and cook for 15 minutes. Toss every 5 minutes. Once ready, remove them into a bowl. Over low heat, melt the butter in a saucepan. Add the vinegar and hot sauce. Stir and cook for a minute.

Turn the heat off. Pour the sauce over the chicken. Toss to coat thoroughly. Transfer the chicken to a serving platter.Serve with a side of celery strips and blue cheese dressing.

Crispy Onion Rings

Prep + Cook Time: 30 minutes | Serves: 4

INGREDIENTS

2 sweet onions
2 cups buttermilk
2 cups pancake mix

2 cups water
1 package cornbread mix
1 tsp salt

DIRECTIONS

Preheat Breville on AirFry function to 370 F and slice the onions into rings. Combine the pancake mix with the water. Line a baking sheet with parchment paper. Dip the rings in the cornbread mixture first, and then in the pancake batter.

Place half of the onion rings onto the sheet and then into the fryer; cook for 8 to 12 minutes, and repeat one more time. Serve with salsa rosa or garlic mayo.

Homemade French Fries

Prep + Cook Time: 25 minutes | Serves: 2

Ingredients

2 russet potatoes, washed, dried, cut strips
2 tbsp olive oil

Salt and freshly ground black pepper to taste

Directions

Spray the Breville Air Fryer basket with cooking spray. In a bowl, toss the strips with olive oil until well-coated, and season with salt and pepper.

Arrange on the Air Fryer basket and cook for 18 minutes at 400 F on AirFry function, turning once halfway through. Check for crispiness and serve immediately, with garlic aioli, ketchup or crumbled cheese.

Buttery Garlic Croutons

Prep + Cook Time: 20 minutes | Serves: 4

Ingredients

2 cups bread, cubed
2 tbsp butter, melted

Garlic salt and black pepper to taste

Directions

In a bowl, toss the bread with butter, garlic salt, and pepper until well-coated. Place the cubes in the Air Fryer basket and cook in the Breville oven for 12 minutes at 380 F on AirFry function, or until golden brown and crispy.

Mac & Cheese Quiche with Greek Yogurt

Prep + Cook Time: 30 minutes | Serves: 4

Ingredients

8 tbsp leftover macaroni with cheese
Extra cheese for serving
Pastry as much needed for forming 4 shells
Salt and black pepper to taste

1 tsp garlic puree
2 tbsp Greek yogurt
2 whole eggs
11¾ oz milk

Directions

Preheat Breville on AirFry function to 360 F on AirFry function. Roll the pastry to form 4 shells. Place them in the Air Fryer pan. In a bowl, mix leftover macaroni with cheese, yogurt, eggs and milk and garlic puree. Pour this mixture over the pastry shells. Top with the cheese evenly. Cook for 20 minutes.

Parsley Mushroom Pilaf

Prep + Cook Time: 40 minutes | Serves: 6

Ingredients

3 tbsp olive oil
4 cups heated vegetable stock
2 cups long-grain rice
1 onion, chopped

2 garlic cloves, minced
2 cups cremini mushrooms, chopped
Salt and ground black pepper to taste
1 tbsp fresh chopped parsley, or to taste

Directions

Preheat Breville on AirFry function to 400 F on AirFry function. Place a frying pan over medium heat. Add oil, onion, garlic, and rice, and cook for 5 minutes. Pour the stock and mushrooms and whisk well. Season with salt and pepper.

Transfer to Air Fryer basket and cook for 20 minutes. Serve sprinkled with chopped parsley.

Air Fryer Chicken Breasts

Prep + Cook Time: 30 minutes | Serves: 4

Ingredients

4 boneless, skinless chicken breasts
1 tsp salt and black pepper

1 tsp garlic powder

Directions

Spray the breasts and the Breville Air Fryer basket with cooking spray. Rub chicken with salt, garlic powder, and black pepper. Arrange the breasts on the basket. Cook for 20 minutes at 360 F on AirFry function, until nice and crispy.

Herby Carrot Cookies

Prep + Cook Time: 30 minutes | Serves: 8

Ingredients

6 carrots, sliced
Salt and black pepper to taste
1 tbsp parsley

1¼ oz oats
1 whole egg, beaten
1 tbsp thyme

Directions

Preheat Breville on Air Fryer function to 360 F. In a saucepan, add carrots and cover with hot water. Cook over medium heat for 10 minutes, until tender. Remove to a plate. Season with salt, pepper, and parsley and mash using a fork. Add the beaten egg, oats, and thyme as you continue mashing to mix well.

Form the batter into cookie shapes. Place in your Air Fryer basket and cook for 15 minutes until edges are browned.

Rosemary Chickpeas

Prep + Cook Time: 20 minutes | Serves: 4

Ingredients

2 (14.5-ounce) cans chickpeas, rinsed, dried
2 tbsp olive oil
1 tsp dried rosemary

½ tsp dried thyme
¼ tsp dried sage
¼ tsp salt

Directions

In a bowl, mix together chickpeas, oil, rosemary, thyme, sage, and salt. Transfer them to the Breville Air Fryer basket and spread in an even layer. Cook for 15 minutes at 380 F on Bake function, shaking once, halfway through cooking.

Chili Beef Sticks

Prep + Cook Time: 2 hrs 10 minutes | Serves: 3

Ingredients

1 lb ground beef
3 tbsp sugar
A pinch garlic powder

A pinch chili powder
Salt to taste
1 tsp liquid smoke

Directions

Place the meat, sugar, garlic powder, chili powder, salt and liquid smoke in a bowl. Mix with a spoon. Mold out 4 sticks with your hands, place them on a plate, and refrigerate for 2 hours. Cook at 350 F for 15 minutes on Bake function, flipping once halfway through.

Spicy Crab Cakes

Prep + Cook Time: 20 minutes | Serves: 6

Ingredients

1 lb crab meat, shredded
2 eggs, beaten
½ cup breadcrumbs
⅓ cup finely chopped green onion
¼ cup parsley, chopped

1 tbsp mayonnaise
1 tsp sweet chili sauce
½ tsp paprika
Salt and black pepper
Olive oil to spray

Directions

In a bowl, add meat, eggs, crumbs, green onion, parsley, mayo, chili sauce, paprika, salt and pepper; mix well. Shape into cakes and grease lightly with oil. Arrange them in the fryer, without overcrowding. Cook for 8 minutes at 400 F on AirFry function, turning once halfway through.

Pumpkin Fritters with Ham & Cheese

Prep + Cook Time: 10 minutes | Serves: 4

INGREDIENTS

1 oz ham, chopped
1 cup dry pancake mix
1 egg
2 tbsp canned puree pumpkin
1 oz cheddar, shredded

½ tsp chili powder
3 tbsp of flour
1 oz beer
2 tbsp scallions, chopped

DIRECTIONS

Preheat Breville on AirFry function to 370 F and in a bowl, combine the pancake mix and chili powder. Mix in the egg, puree pumpkin, beer, shredded cheddar, ham and scallions. Form balls and roll them in the flour. Arrange the balls into the basket and cook for 8 minutes. Drain on paper towel before serving.

Salty Carrot Chips

Prep + Cook Time: 20 minutes | Serves: 2

Ingredients

3 large carrots, washed and peeled

Salt to taste

Directions

Using a mandolin slicer, slice the carrots very thinly heightwise. Put the carrot strips in a bowl and season with salt to taste. Grease the fryer basket lightly with cooking spray, and add the carrot strips. Cook at 350 F for 10 minutes on AirFry function, stirring once halfway through.

Parmesan Cabbage Wedges

Prep + Cook Time: 30 minutes | Serves: 4

INGREDIENTS

½ head of cabbage, cut into 4 wedges
4 tbsp butter, melted
2 cup Parmesan cheese, grated

Salt and black pepper to taste
1 tsp smoked paprika

DIRECTIONS

Preheat Breville on AirFry function to 330 F and line a baking sheet with parchment paper. Brush the butter over the cabbage wedges. Season with salt and pepper.

Coat the cabbage with the Parmesan cheese and arrange on the baking sheet; sprinkle with paprika. Cook for 15 minutes, then flip the wedges over and cook for an additional 10 minutes. Serve with yogurt dip.

Bread Cheese Sticks

Prep + Cook Time: 5 minutes | Serves: 12

Ingredients

6 (6 oz) bread cheese
2 tbsp butter

2 cups panko crumbs

Directions

Put the butter in a bowl and melt in the microwave for 2 minutes; set aside. With a knife, cut the cheese into equal-sized sticks. Brush each stick with butter and dip into panko crumbs. Arrange the sticks in a single layer in the basket. Cook at 390 F for 10 minutes on AirFry function. Flip halfway through, to brown evenly; serve warm.

Lime Pumpkin Wedges

Prep + Cook Time: 30 minutes | Serves: 3

Ingredients

½ pumpkin, washed and cut into wedges
1 tbsp paprika
1 whole lime, squeezed
1 cup paleo dressing

1 tbsp balsamic vinegar
Salt and black pepper to taste
1 tsp turmeric

Directions

Preheat Breville on AirFry function to 360 F. Add the pumpkin wedges in your Air Fryer basket, and cook for 20 minutes. In a mixing bowl, mix lime juice, vinegar, turmeric, salt, pepper and paprika to form a marinade. Pour the marinade over pumpkin, and cook for 5 more minutes.

Rosemary Potato Chips

Prep + Cook Time: 50 minutes | Serves: 3

Ingredients

3 whole potatoes, cut into thin slices
¼ cup olive oil
1 tbsp garlic

½ cup cream
2 tbsp rosemary

Directions

Preheat Breville on AirFry function to 390 F. In a bowl, add oil, garlic and salt to form a marinade. In a separate bowl, add potato slices and top with cold water. Allow sitting for 30 minutes. Drain the slices and transfer to marinade.

Allow sitting for 30 minutes. Lay the potato slices onto the Air Fryer basket and cook for 20 minutes. After 10 minutes, give the chips a turn, sprinkle with rosemary and serve.

Vegetable & Walnut Stuffed Ham Rolls

Prep + Cook Time: 15 minutes | Serves: 4

INGREDIENTS

8 rice leaves
4 carrots
4 slices ham
2 oz walnuts, finely chopped
1 zucchini

1 clove garlic
1 tbsp olive oil
1 tbsp ginger powder
¼ cup basil leaves, finely chopped
Salt and black pepper to taste

DIRECTIONS

In a pan, pour olive oil and add the zucchini, carrots, garlic, ginger and salt; cook for 10 minutes. Stir in basil and walnuts. Soak the rice leaves in warm water. Then fold one side above the filling and roll in. Cook the rolls in the preheated Breville for 8 minutes at 300 F on Bake function.

Sunday Calamari Rings

Prep + Cook Time: 10 minutes | Serves: 4

INGREDIENTS

1 lb calamari (squid), cut in rings
¼ cup flour

2 large beaten eggs
1 cup breadcrumbs

DIRECTIONS

Coat the calamari rings with the flour and dip them in the eggs' mixture. Then, dip in the breadcrumbs. Refrigerate for 2 hours. Line them in the Air Fryer basket and apply oil generously; cook for 9 minutes at 380° F on AirFry function. Serve with garlic mayo and lemon wedges.

Lime Corn with Feta Cheese

Prep + Cook Time: 20 minutes | Serves: 2

INGREDIENTS

2 ears of corn
Juice of 2 small limes

2 tsp paprika
4 oz feta cheese, grated

DIRECTIONS

Preheat Breville on AirFry function to 370 F, peel the corn and remove the silk. Place the corn in the baking pan and cook for 15 minutes. Squeeze the juice of 1 lime on top of each ear of corn. Top with feta cheese.

Mayo Potato Salad with Bacon

Prep + Cook Time: 10 minutes | Serves: 1

Ingredients:

4 lb boiled and cubed potatoes
15 bacon slices, chopped
2 cups shredded cheddar cheese
15 oz sour cream

2 tbsp mayonnaise
1 tsp salt
1 tsp pepper
1 tsp dried herbs, any

DIRECTIONS

Preheat Breville on AirFry function to 350 F, and combine the potatoes, bacon, salt, pepper, and herbs, in a large bowl. Transfer to the Breville baking pan. Cook for about 7 minutes. Remove and stir in sour cream and mayonnaise, to serve.

Scallion & Cheese Sandwich

Prep + Cook Time: 20 minutes | Serves: 1

Ingredients

2 tbsp Parmesan cheese, shredded
2 scallions
2 tbsp butter

2 slices bread
¾ cup cheddar cheese

Directions

Preheat Breville on AirFry function to 360 F. Lay the bread slices on a flat surface. On one slice, spread the exposed side with butter, followed by cheddar and scallions. On the other slice, spread butter and then sprinkle cheese.

Bring the buttered sides together to form sand. Place the sandwich in the cooking basket and cook for 10 minutes. Serve with berry sauce.

Potato Chips with Creamy Lemon Dip

Prep + Cook Time: 25 minutes | Serves: 3

INGREDIENTS

3 large potatoes
1 cup sour cream
2 scallions, white part minced

3 tbsp olive oil.
½ tsp lemon juice
salt and black pepper

DIRECTIONS

Preheat Breville on AirFry function to 350 F and slice the potatoes into thin slices; do not peel them. Soak them in water for 10 minutes, then dry them and spray with oil. Fry the potato slices in two separate batches for 15 minutes; season with salt and pepper.

To prepare the dip, mix the sour cream, olive oil, the scallions, the lemon juice, salt and pepper.

Tasty Bok Choy Crisps

Prep + Cook Time: 10 minutes | Serves: 2

INGREDIENTS

2 tbsp olive oil
4 cups packed bok choy
1 tsp vegan seasoning

1 tbsp yeast flakes
Sea salt, to taste

DIRECTIONS

In a bowl, mix oil, bok choy, yeast and vegan seasoning. Dump the coated kale in the Air fryer basket. Set the temperature of your Breville toaster oven to 360 F on Air Fry function and cook for 5 minutes. Shake after 3 minutes. Serve sprinkled with sea salt.

Cheese Biscuits

Prep + Cook Time: 35 minutes | Serves: 8

Ingredients

½ cup + 1 tbsp butter
2 tbsp sugar
3 cups flour

1 ⅓ cups buttermilk
½ cup Cheddar cheese, grated

Directions

Preheat Breville on AirFry function to 380 F. Lay a parchment paper on a baking plate. In a bowl, mix sugar, flour, ½ cup butter, cheese and buttermilk to form a batter. Make 8 balls from the batter and roll in flour. Place the balls in your Air Fryer basket and flatten into biscuit shapes. Sprinkle cheese and the remaining butter on top. Cook for 30 minutes, tossing every 10 minutes. Serve warm.

Cabbage & Carrot Canapes with Amul Cheese

Prep + Cook Time: 15 minutes | Serves: 2

Ingredients

1 whole cabbage, washed and cut in rounds
1 cube Amul cheese
½ carrot, cubed

¼ onion, cubed
¼ capsicum, cubed
Fresh basil to garnish

Directions

Preheat Breville on AirFry function to 360 F. Using a bowl, mix onion, carrot, capsicum and cheese. Toss to coat everything evenly. Add cabbage rounds to the Air fryer basket. Top with the veggie mixture and cook for 8 minutes. Serve with a garnish of fresh basil.

Garlic Brussels Sprouts

Prep + Cook Time: 25 minutes | Serves: 4

Ingredients

1 block brussels sprouts
½ tsp garlic, chopped
2 tbsp olive oil

½ tsp black pepper
Salt to taste

Directions

Wash the Brussels thoroughly under cold water and trim off the outer leaves, keeping only the head of the sprouts. In a bowl, mix oil and garlic. Season with salt and pepper. Add prepared sprouts to this mixture and let rest for 5 minutes. Place the coated sprouts in the Breville Air Fryer basket and cook for 15 minutes at 380 F.

Cheddar & Prosciutto Croquettes

Prep + Cook Time: 50 minutes | Serves: 6

INGREDIENTS

1 lb cheddar cheese
12 slices of prosciutto
1 cup flour

2 eggs, beaten
4 tbsp olive oil
1 cup breadcrumbs

DIRECTIONS

Cut the cheese into 6 equal pieces. Wrap each piece with 2 prosciutto slices. Place them in the freezer just enough to set. I left mine for about 5 minutes; note that they mustn't be frozen.

Meanwhile, preheat Breville on AirFry function to 390 F, and dip the croquettes into flour first, then in egg, and coat with breadcrumbs. Drizzle the basket with oil and cook the croquettes for 10 minutes, or until golden.

Cheesy Chicken Breasts with Marinara Sauce

Prep + Cook Time: 25 minutes | Serves: 2

Ingredients

2 chicken breasts, skinless, beaten, ½ inch thick
1 egg, beaten
½ cup breadcrumbs
A pinch of salt and black pepper

2 tbsp marinara sauce
2 tbsp Grana Padano cheese, grated
2 slices mozzarella cheese

Directions

Dip the breasts into the egg, then into the crumbs and arrange on the Air fryer basket. Cook for 5 minutes on 400 F on AirFry function. When ready, turn over and drizzle with marinara sauce, Grana Padano and mozzarella cheese. Cook for 5 more minutes. Serve with rice.

Grilled Sandwich with Ham & Cheese

Prep + Cook Time: 15 minutes | Serves: 2

Ingredients

4 slices bread
¼ cup butter

2 slices ham
2 slices cheese

Directions

Preheat Breville on AirFry function to 360 degrees F. Place 2 bread slices on a flat surface. Spread butter on the exposed surfaces. Lay cheese and ham on two of the slices. Cover with the other 2 slices to form sandwiches. Place the sandwiches in the cooking basket and cook for 5 minutes on Bake function. For additional crispiness, set on Toast function for 2 minutes.

Masala Cashew with Mango & Yogurt

Prep + Cook Time: 25 minutes | Serves: 2

Ingredients

8 oz Greek yogurt
2 tbsp mango powder
8¾ oz cashew nuts
Salt and black pepper to taste

1 tsp coriander powder
½ tsp masala powder
½ tsp black pepper powder

Directions

Preheat Breville on AirFry function to 240 F. In a bowl, mix all powders. Season with salt and pepper. Add cashews and toss to coat thoroughly. Place the cashews in your Air Fryer basket and cook for 15 minutes.

French Beans with Shallots & Almonds

Prep + Cook Time: 25 minutes | Serves: 5

Ingredients

1 ½ pounds French beans, washed and drained
1 tbsp salt
1 tbsp pepper

½ pound shallots, chopped
3 tbsp olive oil
½ cup almonds, toasted

Directions

Preheat Breville on AirFry function to 400 F. Put a pan over medium heat, mix beans in hot water and boil until tender, about 5-6 minutes.

Mix the boiled beans with oil, shallots, salt, and pepper. Add the mixture to the cooking basket and cook for 20 minutes. Serve with almonds.

Cheese Scones with Chives

Serves: 10 | Prep + Cook Time: 25 minutes | Serves: 10

Ingredients

6 ¼ oz flour
Salt and black pepper to taste
¾ oz butter
1 tsp chives

1 whole egg
1 tbsp milk
2 ¾ cheddar cheese, shredded

Directions

Preheat Breville on AirFry function to 340 F. In a bowl, mix butter, flour, cheddar cheese, chives, milk and egg to get a sticky dough. Dust a flat surface with flour. Roll the dough into small balls. Place the balls in the cooking basket and cook for 20 minutes. Serve and enjoy!

Paprika Curly Potatoes

Prep + Cook Time: 20 minutes | Serves: 2

Ingredients

2 whole potatoes
1 tbsp extra-virgin olive oil

Salt and black pepper to taste
1 tsp paprika

Directions

Preheat Breville on AirFry function to 350 F. Wash the potatoes thoroughly under cold water and pass them through a spiralizer to get curly shaped potatoes.

Place the potatoes in a bowl and coat with oil. Transfer them to the cooking basket and cook for 15 minutes. Sprinkle a bit of salt and paprika, to serve.

Ham & Mozzarella Pizza with Pineapple

Prep + Cook Time: 15 minutes | Serves: 2

INGREDIENTS

2 tortillas
8 ham slices
8 mozzarella slices

8 thin pineapple slices
2 tbsp tomato sauce
1 tsp dried parsley

DIRECTIONS

Preheat Breville on Pizza function to 330 F and spread the tomato sauce onto the tortillas. Arrange 4 ham slices on each tortilla.

Top the ham with the pineapple, top the pizza with mozzarella and sprinkle with parsley. Cook for 10 minutes and enjoy.

Asparagus Wrapped in Bacon

Serves: 4 | Prep + Cook Time: 25 minutes | Serves: 4

Ingredients

20 spears asparagus
4 bacon slices
1 tbsp olive oil

1 tbsp sesame oil
1 tbsp brown sugar
1 garlic clove, crushed

Directions

Preheat Breville on AirFry function to 380 F. In a bowl, mix the oils, sugar and crushed garlic. Separate the asparagus into 4 bunches (5 spears in 1 bunch) and wrap each bunch with a bacon slice. Coat the bunches with the sugar and oil mix. Place the bunches in your Air Fryer basket and cook for 8 minutes. Serve.

Cajun Shrimp

Prep + Cook Time: 15 minutes | Serves: 3

Ingredients

½ pound shrimp, sauce and deveined
½ tsp Cajun seasoning
Salt as needed

1 tbsp olive oil
¼ tsp black pepper
¼ tsp paprika

Directions

Preheat Breville on AirFry function to 390 F. Using a bowl, make the marinade by mixing paprika, salt, pepper, oil and seasoning. Cut shrimp and cover with marinade. Place the prepared shrimp in the cooking basket and cook for 10-12 minutes, flipping halfway through.

Cheese & Zucchini Cake with Yogurt

Prep + Cook Time: 20 minutes | Serves: 4

Ingredients

1 ½ cups flour
1 tsp cinnamon
3 eggs
2 tsp baking powder
2 tbsp sugar
1 cup milk

2 tbsp butter, melted
1 tbsp yogurt
½ cup shredded zucchini
A pinch of salt
2 tbsp cream cheese

Directions

In a bowl, whisk eggs with sugar, salt, cinnamon, cream cheese, flour, and baking powder. In another bowl, combine all of the liquid ingredients. Gently combine the dry and liquid mixtures.

Stir in zucchini. Line the muffin tins with baking paper, and pour the batter inside them. Arrange on the Air Fryer basket and cook for 15 minutes on Bake function at 380 F.

Classic French Fries

Prep + Cook Time: 35 minutes | Serves: 6

Ingredients

6 medium russet potatoes, sauce
2 tbsp olive oil

Salt to taste

Directions

Cut potatoes into ¼ by 3-inch pieces and place in a bowl with cold water; let soak for 30 minutes. Strain and allow to dry. Preheat Breville on AirFry function to 360 F. Drizzle oil on the dried potatoes and toss to coat. Place the potatoes in the Air Fryer basket and cook for 30 minutes. Season with salt and pepper, to serve.

Amazing Cashew Deligth

Prep + Cook Time: 20 minutes | Serves: 12

Ingredients

3 cups cashews
3 tbsp liquid smoke

2 tsp salt
2 tbsp molasses

Directions

Preheat Breville on AirFry function to 360 F. In a bowl, add salt, liquid, molasses, and cashews; toss to coat thoroughly. Place the cashews in the frying basket and cook for 10 minutes, shaking the basket every 5 minutes.

Healthy Parsnip Fries

Prep + Cook Time: 15 minutes | Serves: 3

INGREDIENTS

4 large parsnips, sliced
¼ cup flour
¼ cup olive oil

¼ cup water
A pinch of salt

DIRECTIONS

Preheat Breville on AirFry function to 390 F. In a bowl, mix the flour, olive oil, water, and parsnip. Mix well and coat. Line the fries in the Air Fryer basket and cook for 15 minutes. Serve with yogurt and garlic paste.

Hearty Eggplant Fries

Prep + Cook Time: 20 minutes Serves: 2

Ingredients

1 eggplant, sliced
1 tsp olive oil

1 tsp soy sauce
Salt to taste

Directions

Preheat Breville on AirFry function to 400 F. Make a marinade of 1 tsp oil, soy sauce and salt. Mix well. Add in the eggplant slices and let stand for 5 minutes. Place the prepared eggplant slices in the cooking basket and cook for 8 minutes. Serve with a drizzle of maple syrup.

Butterbeans with Feta & Bacon

Prep + Cook Time: 10 minutes | Serves: 2

Ingredients

1 (14 oz) can butter beans
1 tbsp chives
3 ½ oz feta

Black pepper to taste
1 tsp olive oil
3 ½ oz bacon, sliced

Directions

Preheat Breville on AirFry function to 340 F. Blend beans, oil and pepper using a blender. Arrange bacon slices on your Air fryer basket. Sprinkle chives on top and cook for 12 minutes. Add feta cheese to the butter bean blend and stir. Serve bacon with the dip.

MEAT RECIPES

Cheddar & Bacon Pulled Pork

Prep + Cook Time: 50 minutes | Serves: 2

Ingredients

½ pork steak
1 tsp steak seasoning
Salt and black pepper to taste
5 thick bacon slices, chopped

1 cup grated Cheddar cheese
½ tbsp Worcestershire sauce
2 bread buns, halved

Directions

Preheat Breville on Bake function to 380 F. Place the pork steak in the baking pan and season with pepper, salt, and the steak seasoning. Cook for 15 minutes, turn, and continue cooking for 6 minutes.

Once ready, remove the steak onto a chopping board and use two forks to shred into pieces. Place the bacon in the Breville baking pan. Cook for 10 minutes. Remove the bacon and stir in the pulled pork, Worcestershire sauce, and the cheddar cheese. Season with salt and pepper.

Place again in the oven and cook for 4 minutes. Slide-out the basket, stir with a spoon, slide the basket back in and cook further for 1 minute. Spoon to scoop the meat into the halved buns and serve with a cheese or tomato dip.

Fried Teriyaki Pork Ribs in Tomato Sauce

Prep + Cook Time: 20 minutes | Serves: 3

Ingredients

1 pound pork ribs
1 tsp salt
1 tsp pepper
1 tbsp sugar
1 tsp ginger juice
1 tsp five-spice powder

1 tbsp teriyaki sauce
1 tbsp light soy sauce
1 garlic clove, minced
2 tbsp honey
1 tbsp water
1 tbsp tomato sauce

Directions

In a bowl, mix pepper, sugar, five-spice powder, salt, ginger juice, teriyaki sauce. Add pork ribs to the marinade and let marinate for 2 hours. Add pork ribs to the basket and cook for 8 minutes on AirFry function at 350 F. In a separate bowl, mix soy sauce, garlic, honey, water, tomato sauce. In a pan over medium heat, heat oil and fry garlic for 30 seconds. Add fried pork ribs and pour the sauce. Stir-fry for a few minutes, serve and enjoy!

Festive Stuffed Pork Chops

Prep + Cook Time: 40 minutes | Serves: 4

Ingredients

8 pork chops
¼ tsp pepper
4 cups stuffing mix
½ tsp salt

2 tbsp olive oil
4 garlic cloves, minced
2 tbsp sage leaves

Directions

Cut a hole in pork chops and fill chops with stuffing mix. In a bowl, mix sage leaves, garlic cloves, oil, salt and pepper. Cover chops with marinade and let sit for 10 minutes. Place the chops in the cooking basket and cook for 25 minutes on AirFry function at 350 F. Serve and enjoy!

Onion & Pork Sausage Balls

Prep + Cook Time: 20 minutes | Serves: 4

Ingredients

3 ½ oz pork sausages, sliced
Salt and black pepper to taste
1 cup onion, chopped

3 tbsp breadcrumbs
½ tsp garlic puree
1 tsp sage

Directions

In a bowl, mix onions, sausages, sage, garlic puree, salt and pepper. In a plate, scatter the breadcrumbs. Form balls out of the mixture and roll in breadcrumbs. Add the balls to the cooking basket and cook for 15 minutes on AirFry function at 340 F. Serve and enjoy!

Maple-Mustard Marinaded Pork Chops

Prep + Cook Time:15 minutes | Serves: 3

Ingredients

3 pork chops, ½-inch thick
Salt and black pepper to taste to season
1 tbsp maple syrup

1 ½ tbsp minced garlic
3 tbsp mustard

Directions

In a bowl, add maple syrup, garlic, mustard, salt, and pepper; mix well. Add the pork and toss it in the mustard sauce to coat well. Slide-out the basket and place the chops inside; cook at 350 F for 6 minutes on AirFry function.

Flip the chops with a spatula and cook further for 6 minutes. Once ready, remove them to a platter and serve with a side of steamed asparagus.

Sweet Pork Belly

Prep + Cook Time: 35 minutes | Serves: 8

Ingredients

2 pounds pork belly
½ tsp pepper
1 tbsp olive oil

1 tbsp salt
3 tbsp honey

Directions

Season the pork belly with salt and pepper. Grease the basket with oil. Add seasoned meat and cook for 15 minutes. Add honey and cook for 10 minutes more at 400 F on AirFry function. Serve with green salad.

Southwest Pork Chops with Caramelized Potatoes

Prep + Cook Time: 45 minutes | Serves: 4

Ingredients

2 tbsp tamarind paste
2 whole caramelized potatoes
1 tbsp garlic, minced
½ cup green mole sauce
3 tbsp corn syrup
1 tbsp olive oil

2 tbsp molasses
4 tbsp southwest seasoning
2 tbsp ketchup
4 pork chops
2 tbsp water

Directions

In a bowl, mix all the ingredients, except for potatoes, pork chops and mole sauce. Let the pork chops marinate in the mixture for 30 minutes. Place pork chops in the basket and cook for 25 minutes on AirFry function at 350 F. Serve with caramelized potatoes and mole sauce.

Easy Pork Chops with Italian Herbs

Prep + Cook Time: 30 minutes | Serves: 4

Ingredients

4 slices pork chops, sliced
2-3 tbsp olive oil
Salt and black pepper to taste
1 whole egg, beaten

1 tbsp flour
Breadcrumbs as needed
A bunch of Italian herbs

Directions

Mix oil, salt, and pepper to form a marinade. Place the beaten egg in a plate. In a separate plate, add the breadcrumbs. Add pork to the marinade and allow to rest for 15 minutes.

Add one slice in egg and then to breadcrumbs; repeat with all slices. Place the prepared slices in the cooking basket and cook for 20 minutes on AirFry function at 400 F. Season with more salt and herbs and serve.

Ratatouille with Pork

Prep + Cook Time: 25 minutes | Serves: 4

Ingredients

4 pork sausages

For Ratatouille
1 pepper, chopped
2 zucchinis, chopped
1 eggplant, chopped
1 medium red onion, chopped
1 tbsp olive oil
1-ounce butterbean, drained

15 oz tomatoes, chopped
2 sprigs fresh thyme
1 tbsp balsamic vinegar
2 garlic cloves, minced
1 red chili, chopped

Directions

Mix pepper, eggplant, oil, onion, zucchinis, and add to the cooking basket. Roast for 20 minutes on Bake function at 390 F. Lower temperature to 350 F. In a saucepan, mix the vegetables and the remaining ratatouille ingredients, and bring to a boil over medium heat.

Let the mixture simmer for 10 minutes; season with salt and pepper. Add sausages to the frying basket and cook for 15 minutes on AirFry function at 350 F. Serve the sausages with ratatouille.

Chipotle Pork Chops with White Rice

Prep + Cook Time: 40 minutes | Serves: 4

Ingredients

2 pork chops
1 lime juice
Salt and black pepper to taste
1 tsp garlic powder
1 ½ cups white rice, cooked
2 tbsp olive oil

1 can (14.5 oz) tomato sauce
1 onion, chopped
3 garlic cloves, minced
½ tsp oregano
1 tsp chipotle chili

Directions

Season pork chops with salt, pepper and garlic powder. In a bowl, mix onion, garlic, chipotle, oregano, and tomato sauce. Add the pork to the mixture. Let marinate for an hour.

Remove meat from the mixture and allow the mixture to sit for 15 minutes. After, place in the basket and cook for 25 minutes on AirFry function at 350 F. Turn once. Serve with rice.

Easy Cocktail Franks Rolls

Prep + Cook Time: 20 minutes | Serves: 4

Ingredients

12 oz cocktail franks

8 oz can crescent rolls

Directions

Use a paper towel to pat the cocktail franks to drain completely. Cut the dough in 1 by 1.5-inch rectangles using a knife. Gently roll the franks in the strips, making sure the ends are visible Place in freezer for 5 minutes.

Preheat Breville oven to 330 F on AirFry function. Take the franks out of the freezer and place them in the frying basket to cook for 8-10 minutes. Increase temperature to 390 F, and cook for another 3 minutes until a fine golden texture appears.

Beer Corned Beef with Carrots

Prep + Cook Time: 35 minutes | Serves: 3

Ingredients

1 tbsp beef spice
1 whole onion, chopped
4 carrots, chopped

12 oz bottle beer
1 ½ cups chicken broth
4 pounds corned beef

Directions

Cover beef with beer and set aside for 20 minutes. Place carrots, onion and beef in a pot and heat over high heat. Add in broth and bring to a boil. Drain boiled meat and veggies; set aside. Top with beef spice. Place the meat and veggies in the cooking basket and cook for 30 minutes at 400 F on AirFry function.

Sweet Pork Meatballs with Cheddar Cheese

Prep + Cook Time: 25 minutes | Serves: 4 to 6

Ingredients

1 lb ground pork
1 large onion, chopped
½ tsp maple syrup
2 tsp mustard

½ cup chopped basil leaves
Salt and black pepper to taste
2 tbsp grated Cheddar cheese

Directions

In a bowl, add ground pork, onion, maple syrup, mustard, basil, salt, pepper, and cheddar cheese; mix well. Form balls. Place in the basket and cook at 400 F for 10 minutes on AirFry function. Shake toss and cook for 5 minutes. Remove them onto a wire rack and serve.

Ham & Cheese Breakfast Sandwich

Prep + Cook Time: 15 minutes | Serves: 4

Ingredients

8 slices whole wheat bread

4 slices lean pork ham

4 slices cheese

8 slices tomato

Directions

Lay four slices of bread on a flat surface. Spread the slices with cheese, tomato, turkey and ham. Cover with the remaining slices to form sandwiches. Add the sandwiches to the cooking basket and cook for 10 minutes at 360 F on AirFry function.

Ham Muffins with Swiss Cheese

Prep + Cook Time: 25 minutes | Serves: 18

Ingredients

5 whole eggs, beaten

2 ¼ oz ham

1 cup milk

¼ tsp pepper

1 ½ cups Swiss cheese, grated

¼ tsp salt

¼ cup green onion, chopped

½ tsp thyme

Directions

Preheat your Breville to 350 F on AirFry function. In a bowl, mix beaten eggs, thyme, onion, salt, Swiss cheese, pepper, and milk. Prepare baking forms and place ham slices in each baking form. Top with the egg mixture. Place the prepared muffin forms in the cooking basket and cook for 15 minutes. Serve and enjoy!

Chinese-Style Broccoli & Beef Steak

Prep + Cook Time: 65 minutes | Serves: 4

Ingredients

¾ lb circular beef steak, cut into strips

1 pound broccoli, cut into florets

⅓ cup oyster sauce

2 tbsp sesame oil

⅓ cup sherry

1 tsp soy sauce

1 tsp white sugar

1 tsp cornstarch

1 tbsp olive oil

1 garlic clove, minced

Directions

In a bowl, mix cornstarch, sherry, oyster sauce, sesame oil, soy sauce, sugar and beef steaks. Set aside for 45 minutes. Add garlic, oil and ginger to the steaks. Place the steaks in the basket and cook for 20 minutes at 390 F on on AirFry function, turning once halfway through.

Pork Sausages Bites with Almonds & Apples

Prep + Cook Time: 40 minutes | Serves: 10

Ingredients

16 oz sausage meat
1 whole egg, beaten
3 ½ oz onion, chopped
2 tbsp dried sage

2 tbsp almonds, chopped
½ tsp pepper
3 ½ oz apple, sliced
½ tsp salt

Directions

Preheat Breville oven to 350 F on AirFry function. In a bowl, mix onion, almonds, apples, egg, pepper and salt. Add the almond mixture and sausages in a Ziploc bag. Mix to coat well and set aside for 15 minutes. From the mixture, form cutlets, add them to frying basket and cook for 25 minutes. Serve with heavy cream and serve.

Allspice Ham with Vanilla Pears

Prep + Cook Time: 30 minutes | Serves: 2

Ingredients

15 oz pears, halved
8 pound smoked ham
1 ½ cups brown sugar
¾ tbsp allspice

1 tbsp apple cider vinegar
1 tsp black pepper
1 tsp vanilla extract

Directions

Preheat your Breville to 330 F on AirFry function. In a bowl, mix pears, brown sugar, cider vinegar, vanilla extract, pepper, and allspice. Place the mixture in a frying pan and fry for 2-3 minutes. Pour the mixture over ham. Add the ham to cooking basket and cook for 15 minutes. Serve ham with hot sauce!

Rosemary Potato with Bacon

Prep + Cook Time: 40 minutes | Serves: 4

Ingredients

4 potatoes, halved
6 garlic cloves, squashed
4 streaky cut rashers bacon

2 sprigs rosemary
1 tbsp olive oil

Directions

In a mixing bowl, mix garlic, bacon, potatoes and rosemary; toss in oil. Place the mixture in the cooking basket and roast for 25-30 minutes at 400 F on AirFry function. Serve and enjoy!

Cheesy Pork Chops with Marinara Sauce

Prep + Cook Time: 15 minutes | Serves: 6

Ingredients

6 pork chops
6 tbsp seasoned breadcrumbs
2 tbsp Parmesan cheese, grated

1 tbsp melted butter
½ cup mozzarella cheese, shredded
1 tbsp marinara sauce

Directions

Grease the cooking basket with cooking spray. In a small bowl, mix breadcrumbs and Parmesan cheese. In another microwave proof bowl, add butter and melt in the microwave.

Brush the pork with butter and dredge into the breadcrumbs. Add pork to the basket and cook for 8 minutes at 400 F on AirFry function. Turn and top with marinara sauce and shredded mozzarella; cook for 5 more minutes.

Pesto & Spinach Stuffed Beef Rolls

Prep + Cook Time: 30 minutes | Serves: 4

Ingredients

2 pounds beef steak, sliced
1 tsp pepper
3 tbsp pesto
1 tsp salt

6 slices cheese
¾ cup spinach, chopped
3 oz bell pepper, deseeded and sliced

Directions

Top the meat with pesto, cheese, spinach, bell pepper. Roll up the slices and secure using a toothpick. Season with salt and pepper accordingly. Place the slices in the basket and cook for 15 minutes on AirFry function at 400 F. Serve immediately!

Mom's Meatballs

Prep + Cook Time: 15 minutes | Serves: 5

Ingredients

1 pound beef, ground
1 tbsp extra-virgin olive oil
1 large red onion, chopped

1 tsp garlic, minced
2 whole eggs, beaten
Salt and black pepper to taste

Directions

In a pan, heat the oil. Add onion and garlic, cook for 1 minute until tender; transfer to a bowl. Add ground beef and egg and mix well. Season with salt and pepper. Roll the mixture golf ball shapes. Place the balls in the frying basket and cook for 4 minutes on AirFry function at 350 F.

POULTRY RECIPES

Chili Chicken Strips & Aioli Sauce

Prep + Cook Time: 15 minutes | Serves: 4

Ingredients

3 chicken breasts, skinless, cut into strips
4 tbsp olive oil
1 cup breadcrumbs
Salt and black pepper to taste
½ tbsp garlic powder

½ tbsp ground chili
Prep + Cook Time½ cup mayonnaise
2 tbsp olive oil
½ tbsp ground chili

Directions

Mix breadcrumbs, salt, pepper, garlic powder and chili, and spread onto a plate. Spray the chicken with oil. Roll the strips in the breadcrumb mixture until well coated. Spray with oil.

Arrange an even layer of strips in the basket and cook for 6 minutes at 360 F on AirFry function, turning once halfway through. To prepare the hot aioli: combine mayo with oil and ground chili. Serve hot.

Mozzarella Chicken Breasts in Marinara Sauce

Prep + Cook Time: 25 minutes | Serves: 2

Ingredients

2 chicken breasts, skinless, beaten, ½-inch thick
1 egg, beaten
½ cup breadcrumbs

A pinch of salt and black pepper
2 tbsp marinara sauce
2 tbsp Grana Padano cheese, grated
2 slices mozzarella cheese

Directions

Dip the breasts into the egg, then into the crumbs and arrange in the basket; cook for 5 minutes at 400 F on AirFry function. Turn and drizzle with marinara sauce, Grana Padano and mozzarella. Cook for 5 more minutes.

Crunchy Chicken Tenderloins

Prep + Cook Time: 15 minutes | Serves: 4

Ingredients

8 chicken tenderloins
2 tbsp butter

2 oz breadcrumbs
1 large egg, whisked

Directions

Preheat Breville on AirFry function to 380 F. Combine butter and breadcrumbs in a bowl. Keep mixing and stirring until the mixture gets crumbly. Dip the chicken in the egg wash. Then dip the chicken in the crumbs mix.

Making sure it is evenly and fully covered; cook for 10 minutes, until crispy. Set on Broil function for crispier taste!

Cheese & Ham Stuffed Turkey Breasts

Prep + Cook Time: 35 minutes | Serves: 4

Ingredients

2 turkey breasts
1 ham slice
1 slice cheddar cheese
2 oz breadcrumbs
1 tbsp cream cheese

1 tbsp garlic powder
1 tbsp thyme
1 tbsp tarragon
1 egg, beaten
Salt and black pepper to taste

Directions

Preheat Breville on AirFry function to 350 F. Cut the turkey in the middle, that way so you can add ingredients in the center. Season with salt, pepper, thyme and tarragon. Combine cream cheese and garlic powder, in a bowl.

Spread the mixture on the inside of the breasts. Place half cheddar slice and half ham slice in the center of each breast. Dip the cordon bleu in egg first, then sprinkle with breadcrumbs. Cook on the tray for 30 minutes.

Chicken Fingers with Plum Sauce

Prep + Cook Time: 8 minutes | Serves: 2

Ingredients

2 chicken breasts, cut in stripes
3 tbsp Parmesan cheese, grated
¼ tbsp fresh chives, chopped
⅓ cup breadcrumbs
1 egg white

2 tbsp plum sauce, optional
½ tbsp fresh thyme, chopped
½ tbsp black pepper
1 tbsp water

Directions

Preheat Breville on AirFry function to 360 F. Mix the chives, Parmesan, thyme, pepper and breadcrumbs. In another bowl, whisk the egg white and mix with the water. Dip the chicken strips into the egg mixture and the breadcrumb mixture. Place the strips in the basket and cook for 10 minutes. Serve with plum sauce.

Homamade Tarragon Chicken

Prep + Cook Time: 15 minutes | Serves: 3

Ingredients

1 boneless and skinless chicken breast
½ tbsp butter
¼ tbsp kosher salt

¼ cup dried tarragon
¼ tbsp black and fresh ground pepper

Directions

Preheat Breville on Bake function to 380 F and place each chicken breast on a 12x12 inches foil wrap. Top the chicken with tarragon and butter; season with salt and pepper to taste. Wrap the foil around the chicken breast in a loose way to create a flow of air. Cook the in the oven for 15 minutes. Carefully unwrap and serve.

Paprika Chicken Breasts with Ham & Cheese

Prep + Cook Time: 40 minutes | Serves: 4

Ingredients

4 skinless and boneless chicken breasts
4 slices ham
4 slices Swiss cheese
3 tbsp all-purpose flour
4 tbsp butter

1 tbsp paprika
1 tbsp chicken bouillon granules
½ cup dry white wine
1 cup heavy whipping cream
1 tbsp cornstarch

Directions

Preheat Breville on AirFry function to 380 F. Pound the chicken breasts and put a slice of ham on each of the chicken breasts. Fold the edges of the chicken over the filling and secure the edges with toothpicks. In a medium bowl, combine the paprika and the flour, and coat the chicken pieces. Fry the chicken for 20 minutes.

In a large skillet, heat the butter and add the bouillon and wine; reduce the heat to low. Remove the chicken from the oven and place in the skillet. Let simmer for around 20-25 minutes.

Bacon-Wrapped Chicken Breasts

Prep + Cook Time: 20 minutes | Serves: 2 to 4

Ingredients

2 chicken breasts
8 oz onion and chive cream cheese
1 tbsp butter
6 turkey bacon

Salt to taste
1 tbsp fresh parsley, chopped
Juice from ½ lemon

Directions

Preheat on AirFry function to 390 F. Stretch out the bacon slightly and lay them in 2 sets; 3 bacon strips together on each side. Place the chicken breast on each bacon set and use a knife to smear cream cheese on both. Share the butter on top and sprinkle with salt. Wrap the bacon around the chicken and secure the ends into the wrap.

Place the wrapped chicken in the basket and cook for 14 minutes. Turn the chicken halfway through. Remove the chicken onto a serving platter and top with parsley and lemon juice. Serve with steamed greens.

Tangy Chicken Drumsticks with Cauliflower

Prep + Cook Time: 50 minutes | Serves: 4

Ingredients

8 chicken drumsticks
2 tbsp oregano
2 tbsp thyme
2 oz oats
¼ cup milk

¼ steamed cauliflower florets
1 egg
1 tbsp ground cayenne
Salt and black pepper to taste

Directions

Preheat Breville on AirFry function to 350 F and season the drumsticks with salt and pepper; rub them with the milk. Place all the other ingredients, except the egg, in a food processor. Process until smooth. Dip each drumstick in the egg first, and then in the oat mixture. Arrange half of them on a baking mat inside the oven. Cook for 20 minutes.

Hot Curried Chicken Wings

Prep + Cook Time: 4 hrs 20 minutes | Serves: 2

Ingredients

8 chicken wings
1 tbsp water
2 tbsp potato starch

2 tbsp cornstarch
2 tbsp hot curry paste
½ tbsp baking powder

Directions

Combine hot curry paste and water, in a small bowl. Place the wings in a large bowl, add the tom yum mixture and coat well. Cover the bowl and refrigerate for 4 hours. Preheat Breville on AirFry function to 370 degrees.

Combine the baking powder, cornstarch and potato starch. Dip each wing in the starch mixture. Place on a lined baking dish in the oven and cook for 7 minutes. Flip over and cook for 5 to 7 minutes more.

Sweet Honey Thighs

Prep + Cook Time: 30 minutes | Serves: 4

Ingredients

4 thighs, skin-on
3 tbsp honey
2 tbsp Dijon mustard

½ tbsp garlic powder
Salt and black pepper to taste

Directions

In a bowl, mix honey, mustard, garlic, salt, and black pepper. Coat the thighs in the mixture and arrange them in the basket. Cook for 16 minutes at 400 F on AirFry function, turning once halfway through.

Tarragon Chicken Tenders

Prep + Cook Time: 15minutes | Serves: 2

Ingredients

2 chicken tenders
Salt and black pepper to taste

½ cup dried tarragon
1 tbsp butter

Directions

Preheat Breville on AirFry function to 390 F. Lay a foil on a flat surface. Place the breasts on the foil, sprinkle the tarragon on both, and share the butter onto both breasts. Sprinkle with salt and pepper.

Wrap the foil around the breasts. Place the wrapped chicken in the basket and cook for 12 minutes. Remove and carefully unwrap. Serve with the sauce extract and steamed veggies.

Chili Lime Whole Chicken

Prep + Cook Time: 50 minutes | Serves: 4

Ingredients

1 (2½ lb) whole chicken, on the bone
Salt and black pepper to taste to season
1 tbsp chili powder
1 tbsp garlic powder
4 tbsp oregano

2 tbsp cilantro powder
2 tbsp cumin powder
2 tbsp olive oil
4 tbsp paprika
1 lime, juiced

Directions

In a bowl, pour the oregano, garlic powder, chili powder, ground cilantro, paprika, cumin powder, pepper, salt, and olive oil. Mix well to create a rub for the chicken, and rub onto it. Refrigerate for 20 minutes.

Preheat Breville on AirFry function to 350 F.

Remove the chicken from the refrigerator; place in basket and cook for 20 minutes. Use a skewer to poke the chicken to ensure that it is clear of juices. If not, cook further for 5 to 10 minutes; let to rest for 10 minutes. Drizzle lime juice over and serve with green salad.

Sweet Asian Chicken Wings

Prep + Cook Time: 15 minutes | Serves: 5

Ingredients

1 pound chicken wings
8 oz flour
8 oz breadcrumbs
3 beaten eggs
4 tbsp Canola oil
Salt and black pepper to taste

2 tbsp sesame seeds
2 tbsp Korean red pepper paste
1 tbsp apple cider vinegar
2 tbsp honey
1 tbsp soy sauce
Sesame seeds, to serve

Directions

Separate the chicken wings into winglets and drumettes. In a bowl, mix salt, oil and pepper. Coat the chicken with beaten eggs followed by breadcrumbs and flour. Place the chicken in the basket. Spray with a bit of oil and cook for 15 minutes on AirFry function at 350 F.

Mix red pepper paste, apple cider vinegar, soy sauce, honey and ¼ cup of water in a saucepan and bring to a boil over medium heat. Transfer the chicken to sauce mixture and toss to coat. Garnish with sesame and serve.

Balsamic Chicken Breast with Avocado & Mango

Prep + Cook Time: 3 hrs 20 minutes | Serves: 2

Ingredients

2 chicken breasts, cubed
1 large mango, cubed
1 medium avocado, sliced
1 red pepper, chopped
5 tbsp balsamic vinegar
15 tbsp olive oil

4 garlic cloves, minced
1 tbsp oregano
1 tbsp parsley, chopped
A pinch of mustard powder
Salt and black pepper to taste

Directions

In a bowl, mix whole mango, garlic, oil, and balsamic vinegar. Add the mixture to a blender and blend well. Pour the liquid over chicken cubes and soak for 3 hours. Take a pastry brush and rub the mixture over breasts as well. Place the chicken cubes in the basket, and cook for 12 minutes on AirFry function at 360 F. Add avocado, mango and pepper and toss well. Drizzle balsamic vinegar and garnish with parsley.

Cayenne Turkey Breasts

Prep + Cook Time: 25 minutes | Serves: 6

Ingredients

3 turkey breasts, boneless and skinless
2 cups panko1 tbsp salt
½ tsp cayenne pepper

½ tbsp black pepper
1 stick butter, melted

Directions

In a bowl, combine the panko, half of the black pepper, cayenne pepper, and half of the salt. In another small bowl, combine the melted butter with salt and pepper. Don't add salt if you use salted butter.

Brush the butter mixture onto turkey breasts. Coat the turkey with the panko mixture. Arrange them on a lined baking dish. Cook for 15 minutes at 390 degrees F. If the turkey breasts are thinner, cook only for 8 minutes.

Herby Turkey Nuggets

Prep + Cook Time: 20 minutes | Serves: 2

Ingredients

8 oz turkey breast, boneless and skinless
1 egg, beaten
1 cup breadcrumbs

1 tbsp dried thyme
½ tbsp dried parsley
Salt and black pepper to taste

Directions

Preheat Breville on AirFry function to 350 F. Mince the turkey in a food processor; transfer to a bowl. Stir in the thyme and parsley, and season with salt and pepper.

Take a nugget-sized ball out of turkey mixture and shape it into a nugget form. Dip in breadcrumbs, then in egg, and in the breadcrumbs again. Place the nuggets on a prepared baking dish, and cook for 10 minutes.

Pineapple & Chicken Kabobs with Sesame Seeds

Prep + Cook Time: 20 minutes | Serves: 4

Ingredients

¾ oz boneless and skinless chicken tenders
½ cup soy sauce
½ cup pineapple juice
¼ cup sesame oil
4 cloves garlic, chopped

1 tbsp fresh ginger, grated
4 scallions, chopped
2 tbsp toasted sesame seeds
1 A pinch of black pepper

Directions

Thread the chicken pieces onto the skewers and trim any fat. In a large-sized bowl, mix the remaining ingredients.

Dip the skewered chicken into the seasoning bowl. Preheat your Breville oven on AirFry function to 390 F. Pat the chicken to dry using a towel and place in the cooking basket. Cook for 7-10 minutes, flipping once. Serve.

Juicy Grilled Chicken

Prep + Cook Time: 25 minutes | Serves: 2

Ingredients

4 chicken breasts, cubed
2 garlic clove, minced
½ cup ketchup
½ tbsp ginger, minced
½ cup soy sauce

2 tbsp sherry
⅓ cup pineapple juice
2 tbsp apple cider vinegar
½ cup brown sugar

Directions

In a bowl, mix in ketchup, pineapple juice, sugar, cider vinegar, ginger. Heat the sauce in a frying pan over low heat. Cover chicken with the soy sauce and sherry; pour the hot sauce on top. Set aside for 15 minutes to marinate.

Place the chicken in the basket and cook for 15 minutes on AirFry function at 360 F.

Mustard Chicken Breasts

Prep + Cook Time: 20 minutes | Serves: 6

Ingredients

¼ cup flour
½ tbsp flour
5 chicken breasts, sliced
1 tbsp Worcestershire sauce
3 tbsp olive oil

¼ cup onions, chopped
1 ½ cups brown sugar
¼ cup yellow mustard
¾ cup water
½ cup ketchup

Directions

In a bowl, mix in flour, salt and pepper. Cover the chicken slices with flour mixture and drizzle oil over the chicken. In another bowl, mix brown sugar, water, ketchup, chopped onion, mustard, Worcestershire sauce and salt.

Dip chicken in the marinade mixture; set aside for 10 minutes. Place the chicken in the basket and cook for 15 minutes at 350 F on AirFry function. Serve immediately.

Chicken Casserole with Coconut

Prep + Cook Time: 20 minutes | Serves: 6

Ingredients

2 large eggs, beaten
2 tbsp garlic powder
1 tbsp salt
½ tbsp ground black pepper

¾ cup breadcrumbs
¾ cup shredded coconut
1 pound chicken tenders

Directions

Preheat your Breville on AirFry function to 400 F. Spray a baking sheet with cooking spray. In a wide dish, whisk in garlic powder, eggs, pepper and salt. In another bowl, mix the breadcrumbs and coconut. Dip your chicken tenders in egg, then in the coconut mix; shake off any excess. Place the prepared chicken tenders in the basket and cook for 12-14 minutes until golden brown.

Honey & Garlic Chicken Drumsticks

Prep + Cook Time: 20 minutes | Serves: 3

Ingredients

2 chicken drumsticks, skin removed
2 tbsp olive oil

2 tbsp honey
½ tbsp garlic, minced

Directions

Add garlic, oil and honey to a sealable zip bag. Add chicken and toss to coat; set aside for 30 minutes. Add the coated chicken to the basket, and cook for 15 minutes at 400 F on AirFry function. Serve and enjoy!

Sweet Sticky Chicken Wings

Prep + Cook Time: 20 minutes | Serves: 4

Ingredients

16 chicken wings
¼ cup butter
¼ cup honey

½ tbsp salt
4 garlic cloves, minced
¾ cup potato starch

Directions

Preheat Breville on AirFry function to 370 F. Rinse and pat dry the wings, and transfer to a bowl. Add the starch to the bowl, and mix to coat the chicken. Place the chicken in a previous greased baking dish. Cook for 5 minutes. Whisk the rest of the ingredients in a bowl. Pour the sauce over the wings and cook for another 10 minutes.

BBQ Chicken Breasts with Pineapple

Prep + Cook Time: 20 minutes | Serves: 2

Ingredients

2 large chicken breasts, cubed
2 green bell peppers, sliced
½ onion, sliced

1 can drain pineapple chunks
½ cup barbecue sauce

Directions

Preheat Breville on Bake function to 370 F. Thread the green bell peppers, the chicken, the onions and the pineapple chunks on the skewers. Brush with barbecue sauce and cook for 20 minutes, until slightly crispy.

Mustard & Thyme Chicken

Prep + Cook Time: 20 minutes | Serves: 4

Ingredients

4 garlic cloves, minced
8 chicken slices
1 tbsp thyme leaves
½ cup dry wine
Salt as needed

½ cup Dijon mustard
2 cups breadcrumbs
2 tbsp melted butter
1 tbsp lemon zest
2 tbsp olive oil

Directions

In a bowl, mix garlic, salt, cloves, breadcrumbs, pepper, oil, butter and lemon zest. In another bowl, mix mustard and wine. Place chicken slices in the wine mixture and then in the crumb mixture. Place the chicken in the basket and cook for 15 minutes at 350 F on AirFry function.

White Wine Chicken Wings

Prep + Cook Time: 30 minutes | Serves: 2

Ingredients

8 chicken wings
½ tbsp sugar
2 tbsp corn flour
½ tbsp white wine

1 tbsp shrimp paste
1 tbsp ginger
½ tbsp olive oil

Directions

In a bowl, mix oil, ginger, wine and sugar. Cover the chicken wings with the prepared marinade and top with flour. Add the floured chicken to shrimp paste and coat it. Place the chicken in the oven and cook for 20 minutes, until crispy on the outside, at 320 F on AirFry function.

Garlic Lemony Chicken Breast

Prep + Cook Time: 20 minutes | Serves: 2

Ingredients

1 chicken breast
2 lemon, juiced and rind reserved
1 tbsp chicken seasoning

1 tbsp garlic puree
A handful of peppercorns
Salt and black pepper to taste

Directions

Place a silver foil sheet on a flat surface. Add all seasonings alongside the lemon rind. Lay the chicken breast onto a chopping board and trim any fat and little bones. Season each side with pepper and salt. Rub the chicken seasoning on both sides well. Place on your silver foil sheet and rub. Seal tightly and flatten with a rolling pin.

Place the breast in the basket and cook for 15 minutes at 350 F on AirFry function. Serve hot.

Crispy Parmesan Escallops

Prep + Cook Time: 10 minutes | Serves: 6

Ingredients

4 skinless chicken breast
2 ½ oz panko breadcrumbs
1 ounce Parmesan cheese, grated

6 sage leaves, chopped
1 ¼ ounce flour
2 beaten eggs

Directions

Place the chicken breasts between a cling film, beat well using a rolling pin until a ½ cm thickness is achieved.

In a bowl, add Parmesan cheese, sage and breadcrumbs. Dredge the chicken into the seasoned flour and dredge into the egg. Finally, dredge into the breadcrumbs. Spray both sides of chicken breasts with cooking spray and cook in the oven for 4-6 minutes, at 350 F on AirFry function, until golden.

Sweet Chinese Chicken Wingettes

Prep + Cook Time: 25 minutes | Serves: 3

Ingredients

1 pound chicken wingettes
1 tbsp cilantro leaves, chopped
Salt and black pepper, to taste
1 tbsp roasted peanuts, chopped
½ tbsp apple cider vinegar

1 garlic clove, minced
½ tbsp chili sauce
1 ginger, minced
1 ½ tbsp soy sauce
2 ½ tbsp honey

Directions

Season chicken with salt and pepper. In a bowl, mix ginger, garlic, chili sauce, honey, soy sauce, cilantro, and vinegar. Cover chicken with honey sauce. Place the prepared chicken to the basket and cook for 20 minutes at 360 F on AirFry function. Serve sprinkled with peanuts.

Honey Chicken Drumsticks

Prep + Cook Time: 20 minutes | Serves: 2

Ingredients

2 chicken drumsticks, skin removed
2 tbsp olive oil

2 tbsp honey
½ tbsp garlic, minced

Directions

Coat all the ingredients in a bowl. Allow to marinate for 30 minutes. Add the chicken to the basket and cook for 15 minutes, shaking once, at 400 F on AirFry function.

Mayo Chicken Breasts with Basil & Cheese

Prep + Cook Time: 20 minutes | Serves: 4

Ingredients

4 chicken breasts, cubed
1 tbsp garlic powder
1 cup mayonnaise
¼ tsp pepper

½ cup soft cheese
½ tbsp salt
Chopped basil for garnish

Directions

In a bowl, mix cheese, mayonnaise, garlic powder and salt to form a marinade. Cover your chicken with the marinade. Place the marinated chicken in the basket and cook for 15 minutes at 380 F on AirFry function. Serve garnished with roughly chopped fresh basil.

Chicken Breasts in Onion-Mushroom Sauce

Prep + Cook Time: 20 minutes | Serves: 4

Ingredients

4 chicken breasts, cubed
1 ½ cup onion soup mix

1 cup mushroom soup
½ cup cream

Directions

Preheat your Breville Air Fryer oven to 400 F on Bake function. Mix mushrooms, onion mix and cream in a bowl. Pour the mixture over chicken and allow to sit for 25 minutes. Place the marinated chicken in the basket and cook for 15 minutes. Serve with remaining cream.

Chicken Wings with Buffalo Sauce

Prep + Cook Time: 35 minutes | Serves: 4

Ingredients

4 pounds chicken wing
½ cup cayenne pepper sauce
½ cup coconut oil

1 tbsp Worcestershire sauce
1 tbsp kosher salt

Directions

In a bowl, combine cayenne pepper sauce, coconut oil, Worcestershire sauce and salt; set aside. Place the chicken in the basket. Cook for 25 minutes at 380 F on Air Fy function. Increase the temperature to 400 F and cook for 5 more minutes. Transfer into a large-sized bowl and toss in the prepared sauce. Serve with celery sticks and enjoy!

Asian-Style Chicken Drumsticks

Prep + Cook Time: 25 minutes | Serves: 4

Ingredients

8 chicken drumsticks
1 tbsp olive oil
1 tbsp sesame oil
4 tbsp honey
3 tbsp light soy sauce

2 crushed garlic cloves
1 small knob fresh ginger, grated
1 small bunch cilantro, chopped
2 tbsp sesame seeds, toasted

Directions

Add all ingredients in a freezer bag, except sesame and coriander. Seal and massage until drumsticks are well coated. Preheat Breville to 400 F on AirFry function. Place the drumsticks in the basket and cook for 10 minutes. Lower temperature to 320 F and cook for 9 more minutes. Sprinkle with sesame seeds and cilantro to serve.

Chicken Wings with Chili-Lime Sauce

Prep + Cook Time: 25 minutes | Serves: 2

Ingredients

10 chicken wings
2 tbsp hot chili sauce

½ tbsp lime juice
Salt and black pepper to serve

Directions

Preheat Breville on AirFry function to 350 F. Mix lime juice and chili sauce. Toss the mixture over the chicken wings. Put the chicken wings in the basket and cook for 25 minutes. Shake every 5 minutes.

Avocado & Radish Chicken Bowl

Prep + Cook Time: 20 minutes | Serves: 2

INGREDIENTS

12 oz chicken breasts
1 avocado, sliced
4 radishes, sliced

1 tbsp chopped parsley
Salt and black pepper to taste

DIRECTIONS

Preheat Breville on AirFry function to 300 degrees F, and cut the chicken into small cubes. Combine all ingredients in a bowl and transfer to a baking dish. Cook for 14 minutes. Serve with cooked rice or fried red kidney beans.

Coconut Chicken Breasts

Prep + Cook Time: 25 minutes | Serves: 4

Ingredients

3 chicken breasts, cubed
Oil as needed
3 cups coconut flakes
3 whole eggs, beaten

½ cup cornstarch
Salt to taste
1 tbsp cayenne pepper
Pepper to taste

Directions

In a bowl, mix salt, cornstarch, cayenne pepper, pepper. In another bowl, add beaten eggs and coconut flakes. Cover chicken with pepper mix. Dredge chicken in the egg mix. Cover chicken with oil. Place the chicken in the basket and cook for 20 minutes at 350 F on AirFry function.

Chicken Wings with Honey & Cashew Cream

Prep + Cook Time: 25 minutes | Serves: 3

Ingredients

1 pound chicken wings
1 tbsp cilantro
Salt and black pepper to taste
1 tbsp cashews cream
1 garlic clove, minced

1 tbsp yogurt
2 tbsp honey
½ tbsp vinegar
½ tbsp ginger, minced
½ tbsp garlic chili sauce

Directions

Preheat Breville on AirFry function to 360 F. Season the wings with salt and pepper, place them in the basket, and cook for 15 minutes. In a bowl, mix the remaining ingredients. Top the chicken with sauce and cook for 5 more minutes.

Chicken & Cheese Enchilada

Prep + Cook Time: 65 minutes | Serves: 6

Ingredients

3 cups chicken breast, chopped
2 cups cheese, grated
½ cup salsa

1 can green chilies, chopped
12 flour tortillas
2 cans enchilada sauce

Directions

In a bowl, mix salsa and enchilada sauce. Toss in the chopped chicken to coat. Place the chicken on the tortillas and roll; top with cheese. Place the prepared tortillas in the basket or on the tray, and cook for 45-50 minutes at 400 F on Bake function. Serve with guacamole and hot dips!

Balsamic Chicken with Mozzarella & Basil

Prep + Cook Time: 25 minutes | Serves: 6

Ingredients

6 chicken breasts, cubed
6 basil leaves
¼ cup balsamic vinegar

6 slices tomato
1 tbsp butter
6 slices mozzarella cheese

Directions

Heat butter and balsamic vinegar in a frying pan over medium heat. Cover the chicken meat with the marinade. Place the chicken in the basket and cook for 20 minutes at 400 F on AirFry function. Top with cheese, and Bake for 1 minute until the cheese melt. Cover with basil, and tomato slices, and serve.

Parmesan Coated Chicken Cutlets

Prep + Cook Time: 30 minutes | Serves: 4

Ingredients

¼ cup Parmesan cheese, grated
4 chicken cutlets
⅛ tbsp paprika
¼ tsp pepper

2 tbsp panko breadcrumbs
1 tbsp parsley
½ tbsp garlic powder
2 large eggs, beaten

Directions

In a bowl, mix Parmesan cheese, breadcrumbs, garlic powder, pepper, paprika and mash the mixture. Add eggs to another bowl. Dip the chicken cutlets in eggs, dredge them in cheese and panko mixture and place them in the basket. Cook for 20-25 minutes on AirFry function at 400 F, or until crispy.

MEATLESS RECIPES

Tomato & Feta Cheese Sandwiches with Pine Nuts

Prep + Cook Time: 60 minutes | Serves: 2

Ingredients

1 heirloom tomato

1 (4- oz) block Feta cheese

1 small red onion, thinly sliced

1 clove garlic

Salt to taste

2 tsp + ¼ cup olive oil

1 ½ tbsp toasted pine nuts

¼ cup chopped parsley

¼ cup grated Parmesan cheese

¼ cup chopped basil

Directions

Add basil, pine nuts, garlic and salt to a food processor. Process while slowly adding ¼ cup of olive oil. Once finished, pour basil pesto into a bowl and refrigerate for 30 minutes. Preheat Breville on AirFry function to 390 F.

Slice the feta cheese and tomato into ½-inch circular slices. Use a kitchen towel to pat the tomatoes dry. Remove the pesto from the fridge and use a spoon to spread some pesto on each slice of tomato. Top with a slice of feta cheese. Add the onion and remaining olive oil in a bowl and toss. Spoon on top of feta cheese.

Place the tomato in the fryer's basket and cook for 12 minutes. Remove to a serving platter, sprinkle lightly with salt and top with the remaining pesto. Serve with rice.

Simple Polenta Crisps

Prep + Cook Time: 80 minutes | Serves: 4

Ingredients

2 cups water

2 cups milk

1 cup instant polenta

Salt and black pepper

fresh thyme, chopped

Directions

Line a tray with paper. Pour water and milk into a saucepan and simmer. Keep whisking as you pour in the polenta. Continue to whisk until polenta thickens and bubbles; season to taste. Add polenta to the lined tray and spread out. Refrigerate for 45 minutes. S

lice, and set polenta into batons and spray with oil. Arrange polenta chips into the basket and cook for 16 minutes at 380 F on AirFry function, turning once halfway through. Make sure the fries are golden and crispy.

Veggie & Garlic Bake

Prep + Cook Time: 30 minutes | Serves: 3

Ingredients

3 turnips, sliced
1 large red onion, cut into rings
1 large zucchini, sliced
Salt and black pepper to taste

2 cloves garlic, crushed
1 bay leaf, cut in 6 pieces
1 tbsp olive oil

Directions

Place the turnips, onion, and zucchini in a bowl. Toss with olive oil and season with salt and pepper.

Preheat Breville on AirFry function to 330 F, and place the veggies into the baking pan. Slip the bay leaves in the different parts of the slices and tuck the garlic cloves in between the slices. Cook for 15 minutes. Serve warm with as a side to a meat dish or salad.

Classic Baked Potatoes

Prep + Cook Time: 30 minutes | Serves: 4

Ingredients

17 oz potatoes
2 garlic cloves, minced
Salt and black pepper to taste

1 tsp rosemary
1 tsp butter

Directions

Wash the potatoes thoroughly under water. Preheat your Breville Oven to 360 F on AirFry function and prick the potatoes with a fork. Place into Air fryer basket and cook for 25 minutes. Cut the potatoes in half and top with butter and rosemary; season with salt and pepper.

Parmesan Cabbage Wedges with Blue Cheese Sauce

Prep + Cook Time: 25 minutes | Serves: 4

Ingredients

½ head cabbage, cut into wedges
2 cups Parmesan cheese, chopped
4 tbsp melted butter

Salt and black pepper to taste
½ cup blue cheese sauce

Directions

Cover cabbage wedges with melted butter, and coat with mozzarella. Place the coated cabbage in the basket and cook for 20 minutes at 380 F on AirFry setting. Serve with blue cheese.

Roasted Butternut Squash with Maple Syrup

Prep + Cook Time: 30 minutes | Serves: 2

Ingredients

1 butternut squash
1 tbsp dried rosemary

2 tbsp maple syrup
Salt to season

Directions

Place the squash on a cutting board and peel. Cut in half and remove the seeds and pulp. Slice into wedges and season with salt. Preheat Breville on AirFry function to 350 F, spray the wedges with cooking spray and sprinkle with rosemary.

Grease the basket with cooking spray and place the wedges in without overlapping. Slide the basket in and cook for 20 minutes, flipping once halfway through. Serve with maple syrup and goat cheese.

Cilantro Roasted Carrots with Cumin Seeds

Prep + Cook Time: 15 minutes | Serves: 6

Ingredients

20 oz carrots, julienned
1 tbsp olive oil

1 tsp cumin seeds
A handful of fresh cilantro

Directions

In a bowl, mix oil, carrots, and cumin seeds. Gently stir to coat the carrots well. Place the carrots in on the lower tray and set to Bake setting at 300 F for 10 minutes. Scatter fresh coriander over the carrots and serve.

Parmesan Coated Green Beans

Prep + Cook Time: 20 minutes | Serves: 6

Ingredients

1 cup panko
2 whole eggs, beaten
½ cup Parmesan cheese, grated
½ cup flour

1 tsp cayenne pepper
1 ½ pounds green beans
Salt to taste

Directions

In a bowl, mix panko, Parmesan cheese, cayenne pepper; season with salt and pepper. Cover the green beans in flour and dip in eggs. Dredge beans in the parmesan-panko mix. Place the prepared beans in the cooking basket and cook for 15 minutes on AirFry function at 350 F. Serve and enjoy!

Tangy Tofu

Prep + Cook Time: 30 minutes | Serves: 2

Ingredients

6 oz extra firm tofu
Black pepper to taste
1 tbsp vegetable broth
1 tbsp soy sauce

⅓ tsp dried oregano
⅓ tsp garlic powder
⅓ tsp dried basil
⅓ tsp onion powder

Directions

Place the tofu on a cutting board, and cut it into 3 lengthwise slices with a knife. Line a side of the cutting board with paper towels, place the tofu on it and cover with a paper towel. Use your hands to press the tofu gently until as much liquid has been extracted from it.

Remove the paper towels and use a knife to chop the tofu into 8 cubes; set aside. In another bowl, add the soy sauce, vegetable broth, oregano, basil, garlic powder, onion powder, and black pepper; mix well with a spoon.

Pour the spice mixture on the tofu, stir the tofu until well coated; set aside to marinate for 10 minutes. Preheat Breville on AirFry function to 390 F, and arrange the tofu in the fryer's basket, in a single layer; cook for 10 minutes, flipping it at the 6-minute mark. Remove to a plate and serve with green salad.

Dill Baby Carrots with Honey

Prep + Cook Time: 20 minutes | Serves: 4

Ingredients

1 pound baby carrots
1 tsp dried dill
1 tbsp olive oil

1 tbsp honey
Salt and black pepper to taste

Directions

Preheat your Breville Oven to 300 F on AirFry function. In a bowl, mix oil, carrots and honey; gently stir to coat the carrots. Season with dill, pepper and salt. Place the carrots in the cooking basket and cook for 15 minutes.

Cheddar & Bean Burritos

Prep + Cook Time: 30 minutes | Serves: 6

Ingredients

6 tortillas
1 cup grated cheddar cheese

1 can (8 oz) beans
1 tsp seasoning, any kind

Directions

Preheat Breville on Bake function to 350 F, and mix the beans with the seasoning. Divide the bean mixture between the tortillas and top with cheddar cheese. Roll the burritos and arrange them on a lined baking dish. Place in the oven and cook for 5 minutes, or to your liking.

Veggie Frittata

Prep + Cook Time: 35 minutes | Serves: 2

Ingredients

1 cup baby spinach
⅓ cup sliced mushrooms
1 large zucchini, sliced with a 1-inch thickness
1 small red onion, sliced
¼ cup chopped chives
¼ lb asparagus, trimmed and sliced thinly

2 tsp olive oil
4 eggs, cracked into a bowl
⅓ cup milk
Salt and black pepper to taste
⅓ cup grated Cheddar cheese
⅓ cup crumbled Feta cheese

Directions

Preheat Breville on Bake function to 320 F and line the baking dish with parchment paper; set aside. In the egg bowl, add milk, salt, and pepper; beat evenly. Place a skillet over medium heat on a stovetop, and heat olive oil.

Add the asparagus, zucchini, onion, mushrooms, and baby spinach; stir-fry for 5 minutes. Pour the veggies into the baking dish and top with the egg mixture. Sprinkle feta and cheddar cheese over and place in the oven. Cook for 15 minutes. Garnish with fresh chives.

Blue Cheese & Pumpkin with Pine Nuts

Prep + Cook Time: 30 minutes | Serves: 1

Ingredients

½ small pumpkin
2 oz blue cheese, cubed
2 tbsp pine nuts
1 tbsp olive oil

½ cup baby spinach, packed
1 spring onion, sliced
1 radish, thinly sliced
1 tsp vinegar

Directions

Preheat Breville on Toast function to 330 F, and place the pine nuts in a baking dish toast them for 5 minutes; set aside. Peel the pumpkin and chop it into small pieces. Place in the baking dish and toss with the olive oil. Increase the temperature to 390 F and cook the pumpkin for 20 minutes.

Place the pumpkin in a serving bowl. Add baby spinach, radish and spring onion; toss with the vinegar. Stir in the cubed blue cheese and top with the toasted pine nuts, to serve.

Veggies Delight

Prep + Cook Time: 30 minutes | Serves: 2

Ingredients

1 parsnip, sliced in a 2-inch thickness
1 cup chopped butternut squash
2 small red onions, cut in wedges
1 cup chopped celery

1 tbsp chopped fresh thyme
Salt and black pepper to taste
2 tsp olive oil

Directions

Preheat Breville on AirFry function to 200 F, and in a bowl, add turnip, squash, red onions, celery, thyme, pepper, salt, and oil; mix well. Add the veggies to the basket and cook for 16 minutes, tossing once halfway through.

Carrot & Chickpea Oat Balls with Cashews

Prep + Cook Time: 30 minutes | Serves: 3

Ingredients

2 tbsp olive oil
2 tbsp soy sauce
1 tbsp flax meal
2 cups cooked chickpeas
½ cup sweet onion, diced
½ cup grated carrots

½ cup roasted cashews
Juice of 1 lemon
½ tsp turmeric
1 tsp cumin
1 tsp garlic powder
1 cup rolled oats

Directions

Combine the oil, onions, and carrots into a baking dish and cook them in AirFry function for 6 minutes at 350 F.

Meanwhile, ground the oats and cashews in a food processor. Place in a large bowl. Process the chickpeas with the lemon juice and soy sauce, until smooth. Add them to the bowl as well.

Add onions and carrots to the bowl with chickpeas. Stir in the remaining ingredients; mix until fully incorporated. Make meatballs out of the mixture. Increase the temperature to 370 degrees F and cook for 12 minutes.

Homemade Blooming Onions

Prep + Cook Time: 40 minutes | Serves: 4

INGREDIENTS

4 onions
4 butter dollops

1 tbsp olive oil

DIRECTIONS

Peel the onions and slice off the root bottom so it can sit well. Cut slices into the onion to make it look like a blooming flower, make sure not to go all the way through; four cuts will do. Preheat Breville on AirFry function to 350 F and place the onions in the oven.

Drizzle with olive oil, place a dollop of butter on top of each onion and cook for about 30 minutes. Serve with garlic mayo dip.

Feta & Scallion Empanadas

Prep + Cook Time: 20 minutes | Serves: 4

Ingredients

4 oz feta cheese
2 sheets filo pastry
1 egg yolk
2 tbsp parsley, finely chopped

1 scallion, finely chopped
2 tbsp olive oil
salt and black pepper

Directions

In a large bowl, beat the yolk and mix with the cheese, the chopped parsley and scallion. Season with salt and black pepper. Cut each filo sheet in three parts or strips. Put a teaspoon of the feta mixture on the bottom.

Roll the strip in a spinning spiral way until the filling of the inside mixture is completely wrapped in a triangle. Preheat Breville on Bake function to 360 F, and brush the surface of filo with oil. Place up to 5 triangles in the oven and cook for 5 minutes. Lower the temperature to 330 F, cook for 3 more minutes or until golden brown.

Zucchini Crisps

Prep + Cook Time: 40 minutes | Serves: 4

Ingredients

4 small zucchini cut lengthwise
½ cup grated Parmesan cheese
½ cup breadcrumbs
¼ cup melted butter

¼ cup chopped parsley
4 garlic cloves, minced
Salt and black pepper to taste

Directions

Preheat Breville on AirFry function to 350 F, and in a bowl, mix breadcrumbs, Parmesan, garlic, and parsley. Season with salt and pepper, to taste; stir in the melted butter. Arrange the zucchinis with the cut side up.

Spread the mixture onto the zucchini. Place h zucchinis in the basket and cook for 13 minutes. Increase the temperature to 370 F, and cook for 3 more minutes. Serve hot.

Tofu & Pea Cauli Rice

Prep + Cook Time: 30 minutes | Serves: 4

Ingredients

Tofu:
½ block tofu
½ cup diced onion
2 tbsp soy sauce

1 tsp turmeric
1 cup diced carrot

Cauliflower:
3 cups cauliflower rice
2 tbsp soy sauce
½ cup chopped broccoli
2 garlic cloves, minced

1 ½ tsp toasted sesame oil
1 tbsp minced ginger
½ cup frozen peas
1 tbsp rice vinegar

Directions

Preheat Breville on AirFry function to 370 F, crumble the tofu and combine it with all tofu ingredients. Place in a baking dish and cook for 10 minutes.

Meanwhile, place all cauli ingredients in a large bowl; mix to combine. Add the cauliflower mixture to the tofu and stir to combine; cook for 12 minutes. Serve.

Cumin Sweet Potatoes Wedges

Prep + Cook Time: 30minutes | Serves: 4

Ingredients

½ tsp salt
½ tsp garlic powder
½ tsp cayenne pepper
¼ tsp cumin

3 tbsp olive oil
3 sweet potatoes, cut into ½-inch thick wedges
A handful of chopped fresh parsley
Sea salt to taste

Directions

In a bowl, mix salt, garlic powder, chili powder, and cumin. Whisk in oil, and coat the potatoes. Arrange in the basket, without overcrowding, and cook for 20 minutes at 380 F on AirFry function. Toss every 5 minutes. Sprinkle with parsley and sea salt and serve.

Eggplant Patties with Mozzarella

Prep + Cook Time: 10 minutes | Serves: 1

Ingredients

1 hamburger bun
2-inch eggplant slices, cut along the round axis

1 mozzarella slice
1 red onion cut into 3 rings

1 lettuce leaf   1 pickle, sliced
½ tbsp tomato sauce

Directions

Preheat Breville on Bake function to 330 F, and cook the eggplant slices to roast for 6 minutes. Place the mozzarella slice on top of the eggplant and cook for 30 more seconds. Spread tomato sauce on one half of the bun.

Place the lettuce leaf on top of the sauce. Place the cheesy eggplant on top of the lettuce. Top with onion rings and pickles, and then with the other bun half and enjoy.

Spinach Enchiladas with Mozzarella

Prep + Cook Time: 20 minutes | Serves: 4

Ingredients

8 corn tortillas   ½ cup sliced onions
2 cups mozzarella cheese, shredded   ½ cup sour cream
1 cup ricotta cheese   1 tbsp butter
1 package frozen spinach   1 can enchilada sauce
1 garlic clove, minced

Directions

In a saucepan, heat oil and sauté garlic and onion, until brown. Stir in the frozen spinach and cook for 5 more minutes. Remove from the heat and stir in the ricotta cheese, sour cream and the shredded cheese.

Warm the tortillas on low heat for 15 seconds in the oven. Spoon ¼ cup of spinach mixture in the middle of a tortilla. Roll up and place seam side down in the basket. Pour the enchilada sauce over the tortillas and sprinkle with the remaining cheese. Cook for 15 minutes at 380 F on AirFry function, turning once halfway through.

Chili Sweet Potato Fries

Prep + Cook Time: 30 minutes | Serves: 4

Ingredients

½ tsp salt   ¼ tsp cumin
½ tsp garlic powder   3 tbsp olive oil
½ tsp chili powder   3 sweet potatoes, cut into thick strips

Directions

In a bowl, mix salt, garlic powder, chili, and cumin, and whisk in oil. Coat the strips well in this mixture and arrange them in the basket, without overcrowding. Cook for 20 minutes at 380 F on AirFry function, or until crispy.

Chinese Spring Rolls

Prep + Cook Time: 15 minutes | Serves: 4

Ingredients

½ cabbage, grated
2 carrots, grated
1 tsp minced ginger
1 tsp minced garlic
1 tsp sesame oil

1 tsp soy sauce
1 tsp sesame seeds
½ tsp salt
1 tsp olive oil
1 package spring roll wrappers

Directions

Combine all ingredients in a bowl. Divide the mixture between the spring roll sheets, and roll them up; arrange on the baking tray. Cook in the oven for 5 minutes on Bake function at 370 F.

Cheese & Vegetable Pizza

Prep + Cook Time: 15 minutes | Serves: 1

Ingredients

1 ½ tbsp tomato paste
¼ cup grated cheddar cheese
¼ cup grated mozzarella cheese
1 tbsp cooked sweet corn
4 zucchini slices
4 eggplant slices

4 red onion rings
½ green bell pepper, chopped
3 cherry tomatoes, quartered
1 tortilla
¼ tsp basil
¼ tsp oregano

Directions

Preheat Breville on Pizza function to 350 F, and spread the tomato paste on the tortilla. Arrange the zucchini and eggplant slices first, then green peppers, and onion rings. Arrange the cherry tomatoes and scatter the corn. Sprinkle with oregano and basil, and top with cheddar and mozzarella. Cook for 10-12 minutes.

Masala Vegetable Skewers

Prep + Cook Time: 20 minutes | Serves: 4

Ingredients

2 tbsp cornflour
1 cup canned beans
⅓ cup grated carrots
2 boiled and mashed potatoes
¼ cup chopped fresh mint leaves
½ tsp garam masala powder

½ cup paneer
1 green chili
1-inch piece of fresh ginger
3 garlic cloves
Salt to taste

Directions

Soak 12 skewers until ready to use. Preheat Breville on AirFry function to 390 F, and place the beans, carrots, garlic, ginger, chili, paneer, and mint, in a food processor; process until smooth, then transfer to a bowl.

Add the mashed potatoes, corn flour, salt, and garam masala powder to the bowl; mix until fully incorporated. Divide the mixture into 12 equal pieces. Shape each of the pieces around a skewer. Cook skewers for 10 minutes.

Veggie Gratin

Prep + Cook Time: 30 minutes | Serves: 2 to 3

Ingredients

1 cup cubed eggplant
¼ cup chopped red pepper
¼ cup chopped green pepper
¼ cup chopped onion
⅓ cup chopped tomatoes
1 clove garlic, minced
1 tbsp sliced pimiento-stuffed olives

1 tsp capers
¼ tsp dried basil
¼ tsp dried marjoram
Salt and black pepper to taste
¼ cup grated mozzarella cheese
1 tbsp breadcrumbs

Directions

In a bowl, add eggplant, green and peppers, onion, tomatoes, olives, garlic, basil, marjoram, capers, salt, and black pepper. Lightly grease the tray with cooking spray.

Ladle the eggplant mixture into the baking tray and level it using the vessel. Sprinkle mozzarella cheese on top and cover with breadcrumbs. Place the dish in the oven and cook for 20 minutes on Bake function at 320 F.

Nutmeg Broccoli with Eggs & Cheddar Cheese

Prep + Cook Time: 15 minutes | Serves: 4

Ingredients

1 lb broccoli
4 eggs
1 cup cheddar cheese, shredded
1 cup cream

1 pinch nutmeg
1 tsp ginger powder
Salt and black pepper to taste

Directions

In boiling water, steam the broccoli for 5 minutes. Drain them and add 1 egg, cream, nutmeg, ginger, salt and pepper. Butter small ramekins and spread the mixture. Sprinkle the shredded cheese on top. Cook for 10 minutes at 280 F on AirFry function.

Veggie Mix Fried Chips

Prep + Cook Time: 45 minutes | Serves: 4

Ingredients

1 large eggplant
5 potatoes
3 zucchinis
½ cup cornstarch

½ cup water
½ cup olive oil
Salt to season

Directions

Preheat Breville on AirFry function to 390 F, and cut the eggplant and zucchini in long 3-inch strips. Peel and cut the potatoes into 3-inch strips; set aside. In a bowl, stir in cornstarch, water, salt, pepper, oil, eggplants, zucchini, and potatoes. Place one-third of the veggie strips in the basket and cook for 12 minutes. Once ready, transfer them to a serving platter. Repeat the cooking process for the remaining veggie strips. Serve warm.

Cheese Stuffed Green Peppers with Tomato Sauce

Prep + Cook Time: 35 minutes | Serves: 4

Ingredients

2 cans green chili peppers
1 cup cheddar cheese, shredded
1 cup Monterey Jack cheese
2 tbsp all-purpose flour

2 large eggs, beaten
½ cup milk
1 can tomato sauce

Directions

Preheat Breville on AirFry function to 380 F, and spray a baking dish with cooking spray. Take half of the chilies and arrange them in the baking dish. Top with half of the cheese and cover with the other half of the chilies.

In a medium bowl, combine the eggs, the milk, the flour and pour the mixture over the chilies. Cook for 20 minutes. Remove the chilies and pour the tomato sauce over them; cook for 15 minutes. Remove from oven fryer and top with the remaining cheese.

Grandma´s Ratatouille

Prep + Cook Time: 30 minutes | Serves: 2

Ingredients

1 tbsp olive oil
3 roma tomatoes, thinly sliced
2 garlic cloves, minced
1 zucchini, thinly sliced

2 yellow bell peppers, sliced
1 tbsp vinegar
2 tbsp herbs de Provence
Salt and black pepper to taste

Directions

Preheat Breville on AirFry function to 390 F, and place all ingredients in a bowl. Season with salt and pepper, and stir until the veggies are well coated. Arrange the vegetable in a round baking dish and place in the oven. Cook for 15 minutes, shaking occasionally. Let sit for 5 more minutes after the timer goes off.

Balsamic Eggplant Caviar

Prep + Cook Time: 20 minutes | Serves: 3

Ingredients

3 medium eggplants
½ red onion, chopped and blended
2 tbsp balsamic vinegar

1 tbsp olive oil
Salt

Directions

Arrange the eggplants in the basket and cook them for 15 minutes at 380 F on Bake function. Remove and let them cool. Then cut the eggplants in half, lengthwise, and empty their insides with a spoon.

Blend the onion in a blender. Put the inside of the eggplants in the blender and process everything. Add the vinegar, olive oil and salt, then blend again. Serve cool with bread and tomato sauce or ketchup.

Buttom Mushrooms Stuffed with Tempeh & Cheddar

Prep + Cook Time: 20 minutes | Serves: 3 to 4

Ingredients

14 small button mushrooms
1 clove garlic, minced
Salt and pepper to taste
4 slices tempeh, chopped

¼ cup grated Cheddar cheese
1 tbsp olive oil
1 tbsp chopped parsley

Directions

Preheat on AirFry function to 390 F, and in a bowl, add the oil, tempeh, cheddar cheese, parsley, salt, pepper, and garlic. Mix well with a spoon. Cut the stalks of the mushrooms off and fill each cap with the tempeh mixture.

Press the tempeh mixture into the caps to avoid from falling off. Place the stuffed mushrooms in the basket and cook at 390 F for 8 minutes. Once golden and crispy, plate them and serve with a green salad.

Spinach Balls with Ricotta

Prep + Cook Time: 20 minutes | Serves: 4

Ingredients

14 oz store-bought crescent dough
1 cup steamed spinach
1 cup crumbled ricotta cheese

¼ tsp garlic powder
1 tsp chopped oregano
¼ tsp salt

Directions

Preheat Breville on AirFry function to 350 F, and roll the dough onto a lightly floured flat surface. Combine the ricotta, spinach, oregano, salt, and garlic powder together in a bowl. Cut the dough into 4 equal pieces.

Divide the spinach/feta mixture between the dough pieces. Make sure to place the filling in the center. Fold the dough and secure with a fork. Place onto a lined baking dish, and then in the oven. Cook for 12 minutes, until lightly browned.

Cabbage Steaks with Fennel Seeds

Prep + Cook Time: 25 minutes | Serves: 3

Ingredients

1 cabbage head
1 tbsp garlic paste
1 tsp salt

2 tbsp olive oil
½ tsp black pepper
2 tsp fennel seeds

Directions

Preheat Breville on AirFry function to 350 F, and slice the cabbage into 1 ½-inch slice. In a small bowl, combine all the other ingredients; brush cabbage with the mixture. Arrange the steaks in the oven and cook for 15 minutes.

Vegan Beetroot Chips

Prep + Cook Time: 9 minutes | Serves: 2

Ingredients

4 cups golden beetroot, sliced
2 tbsp olive oil
1 tbsp yeast flakes

1 tsp vegan seasoning
Salt to taste

Directions

In a bowl, add the oil, beetroot, the vegan seasoning, and the yeast and mix well. Dump the coated chips in the basket. Set the heat to 370 F and cook on AirFry function for a total of 6 minutes, shaking once halfway through.

Cheese Ravioli Lunch

Prep + Cook Time: 15 minutes | Serves: 6

Ingredients

1 package cheese ravioli
2 cup Italian breadcrumbs
¼ cup Parmesan cheese, grated

1 cup buttermilk
1 tsp olive oil
¼ tsp garlic powder

Directions

Preheat Breville on AirFry function to 390 F, and in a small bowl, combine breadcrumbs, Parmesan cheese, garlic powder, and olive oil. Dip the ravioli in the buttermilk and then coat them with the breadcrumb mixture.

Line a baking sheet with parchment paper and arrange the ravioli on it. Place in the oven and cook for 5 minutes. Serve the air-fried ravioli with marinara jar sauce.

Carrots & Shallots with Yogurt

Prep + Cook Time: 25 minutes | Serves: 4

Ingredients

2 tsp olive oil
2 shallots, chopped
3 carrots, sliced
Salt to taste

¼ cup yogurt
2 garlic cloves, minced
3 tbsp parsley, chopped

Directions

In a bowl, mix sliced carrots, salt, garlic, shallots, parsley and yogurt. Sprinkle with oil. Place the veggies in your basket and cook for 15 minutes on AirFry function at 370 F. Serve with basil and garlic mayo.

Potato Fries with Ketchup

Prep + Cook Time: 20 minutes | Serves: 2

Ingredients

2 potatoes
1 tbsp tomato ketchup
2 tbsp olive oil

Salt and black pepper to taste
2 tbsp coconut oil

Directions

Use a spiralizer to spiralize the potatoes. In a bowl, mix oil, coconut oil, salt and pepper. Cover the potatoes with the oil mixture. Place the potatoes in the basket and cook for 15 minutes on AirFry function at 360 F. Serve with ketchup, mayonnaise or black and enjoy.

FISH & SEAFOOD

Basil Fish with Pine Nuts

Prep + Cook Time: 15 minutes | Serves: 6

Ingredients

1 bunch of basil
2 garlic cloves, minced
1 tbsp olive oil
1 tbsp Parmesan cheese, grated

Black pepper and salt to taste
2 tbsp Pine nuts
6 white fish fillet
2 tbsp olive oil

Directions

Season the fillets with salt and pepper. Preheat Breville on AirFry function to 350 F, and cook the fillets inside for 8 minutes. In a bowl, add basil, oil, pine nuts, garlic and Parmesan cheese; mix with hand. Serve with the fish.

Saucy Cod Fish with Green Onions

Prep + Cook Time: 20 minutes | Serves: 4

Ingredients

7 ¼ oz cod fish fillets
4 tbsp chopped cilantro
Salt to taste
A handful of green onions, chopped
1 cup water

5 slices of ginger
5 tbsp light soy sauce
3 tbsp oil
1 tsp dark soy sauce
5 cubes rock sugar

Directions

Cover cod fish with salt and coriander; drizzle with oil. Place the fish fillet in the cooking basket and cook for 15 minutes at 360 F on AirFry function. Place the remaining ingredients in a frying pan over medium heat; cook for 5 minutes. Serve the fish with the sauce.

Parmesan Tilapia Fillets

Prep + Cook Time: 15 minutes | Serves: 4

Ingredients

¾ cup grated Parmesan cheese
1 tbsp olive oil
2 tsp paprika
1 tbsp chopped parsley

¼ tsp garlic powder
¼ tsp salt
4 tilapia fillets

Directions

Preheat Breville on AirFry function to 350 F, and mix parsley, Parmesan cheese, garlic, salt, and paprika in a shallow bowl. Brush the olive oil over the fillets, and then coat them with the Parmesan mixture. Place tilapia onto a lined baking sheet, and then into the oven. Cook for 8-10 minutes on all sides.

Old Bay Shrimp

Prep + Cook Time: 10 minutes | Serves: 2 to 3

Ingredients

1 lb jumbo shrimp
Salt to taste
¼ tsp old bay seasoning

⅓ tsp smoked paprika
¼ tsp chili powder
1 tbsp olive oil

Directions

Preheat Breville on AirFry function to 390 F. In a bowl, add the shrimp, paprika, oil, salt, old bay seasoning, and chili powder; mix well. Place the shrimp in the oven, and cook for 5 minutes.

Parsley Catfish Fillets

Prep + Cook Time: 25 minutes | Serves: 4

Ingredients

4 catfish fillets, rinsed and dried
¼ cup seasoned fish fry

1 tbsp olive oil
1 tbsp parsley, chopped

Directions

Add seasoned fish fry, and fillets in a large Ziploc bag; massage well to coat. Place the fillets in your Breville Air Fryer basket and cook for 10 minutes at 360 F on AirFry function. Flip the fish and cook for 2-3 more minutes. Top with parsley and serve.

Buttery Crab Legs

Prep + Cook Time: 15 minutes | Serves: 3

Ingredients

3 pounds crab legs
2 cups butter

1 cup salted water

Directions

Preheat Breville on AirFry function to 380 F, and dip the crab legs in salted water; let stay for a few minutes. Place the legs in the basket and cook for 10 minutes. Melt the butter in the microwave. Pour over crab legs and serve.

Party Cod Nuggets

Prep + Cook Time: 25 minutes | Serves: 4

Ingredients

1 ¼ lb cod fillets, cut into 4 to 6 chunks each
½ cup flour
1 egg
1 tbsp water

1 cup cornflakes
1 tbsp olive oil
Salt and black pepper to taste

Directions

Place the oil and cornflakes in a food processor and process until crumbed. Season the fish chunks with salt and pepper. In a bowl, beat the egg along with water. Dredge the chunks in flour first, then dip in the egg, and coat with cornflakes. Arrange on a lined sheet, and cook on AirFry function at 350 F for 15 minutes, until crispy.

Smoked Paprika Tiger Shrimp

Prep + Cook Time: 10 minutes | Serves: 4

Ingredients

5-6 oz tiger shrimp, 12 to 16 pieces
1 tbsp olive oil
½ a tbsp old bay seasoning

¼ a tbsp cayenne pepper
¼ a tbsp smoked paprika
A pinch of sea salt

Directions

Preheat Breville on AirFry function to 380 F, and mix all ingredients in a large bowl. Coat the shrimp with a little bit of oil and spices. Place the shrimp in the frying basket and fry for 6-7 minutes. Serve with rice or salad.

Crusty Scallops

Prep + Cook Time: 5 minutes | Serves: 6

Ingredients

12 fresh scallops
3 tbsp flour
4 salt and black pepper

1 egg, lightly beaten
1 cup breadcrumbs

Directions

Coat the scallops with flour. Dip into the egg, then into the breadcrumbs. Spray them with olive oil and arrange them in the oven. Cook for 6 minutes at 360 F on AirFry function, turning once halfway through cooking.

Rosemary & Garlic Prawns

Prep + Cook Time: 1 h 15 minutes | Serves: 2

Ingredients

8 large prawns
3 garlic cloves, minced
1 rosemary sprig, chopped

½ tbsp melted butter
Salt and black pepper to taste

Directions

Combine garlic, butter, rosemary, salt and pepper, in a bowl. Add the prawns to the bowl and mix to coat them well. Cover the bowl and refrigerate for an hour. Preheat Breville on AirFry function to 350 F, and cook for 6 minutes. Increase the temperature to 390 degrees, and cook for one more minute.

Lemon Salmon

Prep + Cook Time: 20 minutes | Serves: 2

Ingredients

2 salmon fillets
Salt, to taste

Zest of a lemon

Directions

Spray the fillets with olive oil and rub them with salt and lemon zest. Line baking paper in the basket to avoid sticking. Cook the fillets for 10 minutes at 360 F on AirFry function, turning once halfway through. Serve with steamed asparagus and a drizzle of lemon juice.

Lobster Tails with Lemon-Garlic Sauce

Prep + Cook Time: 15 minutes | Serves: 3

Ingredients

4 oz lobster tails
1 tsp garlic, minced
1 tbsp butter

Salt and black pepper to taste
½ tbsp lemon Juice

Directions

Add all the ingredients to a food processor, except for shrimp, and blend well. Wash lobster and halve using meat knife; clean the skin of the lobster and cover with the marinade. Preheat your Breville to 380 F.

Place the lobster in the cooking basket and cook for 10 minutes on AirFry function. Serve with fresh herbs.

Savory Shrimp Bowl

Prep + Cook Time: 15 minutes | Serves: 6

Ingredients

1 ¼ pound tiger shrimp
¼ tsp cayenne pepper
½ tsp old bay seasoning

¼ tsp smoked paprika
A pinch of salt
1 tbsp olive oil

Directions

Preheat your Breville oven to 390 F on AirFry function. In a bowl, mix all listed ingredients. Place the mixture in your the cooking basket and cook for 5 minutes. Serve with warm rice and a drizzle of lemon juice.

Citrus Cilantro Catfish

Prep + Cook Time: 20 minutes | Serves: 2

Ingredients

2 catfish fillets
2 tsp blackening seasoning
Juice of 1 lime

2 tbsp butter, melted
1 garlic clove, mashed
2 tbsp cilantro

Directions

In a bowl, blend in garlic, lime juice, cilantro and butter. Divide the sauce into two parts, pour 1 part of the sauce over your fillets; cover the fillets with seasoning. Place the fillets in the basket and cook for 15 minutes at 360 F on AirFry function. Serve the cooked fish with remaining sauce.

Salmon & Caper Cakes

Prep + Cook Time: 15 minutes | Serves: 2

Ingredients

8 oz salmon, cooked
1 ½ oz potatoes, mashed
A handful of capers

A handful of parsley, chopped
Zest of 1 lemon
1 ¾ oz plain flour

Directions

Carefully flake the salmon. In a bowl, mix flaked salmon, zest, capers, dill, and mashed potatoes. Form small cakes using the mixture and dust the cakes with flour; refrigerate for 60 minutes. Preheat your Breville to 350 F and cook the cakes for 10 minutes on AirFry function. Serve chilled.

Breaded Seafood

Prep + Cook Time: 15 minutes | Serves: 4

Ingredients

1 lb scallops, mussels, fish fillets, prawns, shrimp
2 eggs, lightly beaten

Salt and black pepper
1 cup breadcrumbs mixed with zest of 1 lemon

Directions

Clean the seafood as needed. Dip each piece into the egg; and season with salt and pepper. Coat in the crumbs and spray with oil. Arrange into the frying basket and cook for 10 minutes at 400 F on AirFry function, turning once halfway through.

Lemon Pepper Tilapia Fillets

Prep + Cook Time: 15 minutes | Serves: 4

Ingredients

1 pound tilapia fillets
1 tbsp old bay seasoning
2 tbsp canola oil

2 tbsp lemon pepper
Salt to taste
2-3 butter buds

Directions

Preheat your Breville oven to 400 F on Bake function, and drizzle tilapia fillets with canola oil. In a bowl, mix salt, lemon pepper, butter buds, and seasoning; spread on the fish. Place the fillet on the tray and cook for 10 minutes, until tender and crispy.

Cajun Salmon with Lemon

Prep + Cook Time: 10 minutes | Serves: 1

Ingredients

1 salmon fillet
¼ tsp brown sugar
Juice of ½ lemon

1 tbsp cajun seasoning
2 lemon wedges
1 tbsp chopped parsley, for garnishing

Directions

Preheat Breville on Bake function to 350 F, and combine sugar and lemon; coat the salmon with this mixture. Coat with the Cajun seasoning as well. Place a parchment paper on the tray and cook the fish for 10 minutes. Serve with lemon wedges and chopped parsley.

BREAKFAST

Banana Cake with Peanut Butter

Prep + Cook Time: 50 minutes | Serves: 2

Ingredients

1 cup plus
1 tbsp flour
¼ tsp baking soda
1 tsp baking powder
⅓ cup sugar
2 mashed bananas
¼ cup vegetable oil

1 egg, beaten
1 tsp vanilla extract
¾ cup chopped walnuts
¼ tsp salt
2 tbsp peanut butter
2 tbsp sour cream
 for greasing

Directions

Preheat Breville on AirFry function to 330 degrees F. Spray the Breville baking pan with cooking spray or grease with butter. Combine the flour, salt, baking powder, and baking soda, in a bowl.

In another bowl, combine bananas, oil, egg, peanut butter, vanilla, sugar, and sour cream. Combine both mixtures gently. Stir in the chopped walnuts. Pour the batter into the dish. Cook for 40 minutes. Serve cool.

Apricot & Almond Scones

Prep + Cook Time: 30 minutes | Serves: 4

Ingredients

2 cups flour
 ⅓ cup sugar
2 tsp baking powder
½ cup sliced almonds
¾ cup chopped dried apricots

¼ cup cold butter, cut into cubes
½ cup milk
1 egg
1 tsp vanilla extract

Directions

Line the Breville Air Fryer basket with baking paper. Mix together flour, sugar, baking powder, almonds and apricots. Rub the butter into the dry ingredients with hands to form a sandy, crumbly texture. Whisk together egg, milk and vanilla extract.

Pour into the dry ingredients and stir to combine. Sprinkle a working board with flour, lay the dough onto the board and give it a few kneads. Shape into a rectangle and cut into 8 squares. Arrange the squares on the basket and cook for 14 minutes at 390 F on Bake function.

Lemon Cupcakes with Orange Yogurt Frost

Prep + Cook Time: 25 minutes | Serves: 5

Ingredients

Lemon Frosting:
1 cup natural yogurt
Sugar to taste
1 orange, juiced

1 tbsp orange zest
7 oz cream cheese

Cupcake:
2 lemons, quartered
½ cup flour + extra for basing
¼ tsp salt
2 tbsp sugar
1 tsp baking powder

1 tsp vanilla extract
2 eggs
½ cup softened butter
2 tbsp milk

Directions

In a bowl, add the yogurt and cream cheese. Mix until smooth. Add the orange juice and zest; mix well. Gradually add the sweetener to your taste while stirring until smooth. Make sure the frost is not runny. Set aside.

For cupcakes: Place the lemon quarters in a food processor and process it until pureed. Add the baking powder, softened butter, milk, eggs, vanilla extract, sugar, and salt. Process again until smooth.

Preheat Breville on Bake function to 400 F. Flour the bottom of 10 cupcake cases and spoon the batter into the cases ¾ way up. Place them in the Air Fryer basket and bake for 7 minutes. Once ready, remove and let cool. Design the cupcakes with the frosting.

Parmesan Asparagus

Prep + Cook Time: 30 minutes | Serves: 6

INGREDIENTS

1 lb. asparagus spears
¼ cup flour
1 cup breadcrumbs

½ cup Parmesan cheese, grated
2 eggs, beaten
Salt and black pepper to taste

DIRECTIONS

Preheat Breville on AirFry function to 370 F and combine the breadcrumbs and Parmesan, in a small bowl. Season with salt and pepper. Line a baking sheet with parchment paper. Dip half of the spears into the flour first, then into the eggs, and finally coat with crumbs.

Arrange them on the sheet and bake for about 8 to 10 minutes. Repeat with the other half of the spears. Serve with melted butter, hollandaise sauce or freshly squeezed lemon.

Vanilla Raspeberry Pancakes with Maple Syrup

Prep + Cook Time: 15 minutes | Serves: 4

Ingredients

2 cups all-purpose flour
1 cup milk
3 eggs, beaten
1 tsp baking powder
1 cup brown sugar

1 ½ tsp vanilla extract
½ cup frozen raspberries, thawed
2 tbsp maple syrup
A pinch of salt
for greasing

Directions

Preheat Breville on Bake function to 390 F. In a bowl, mix the flour, baking powder, salt, milk, eggs, vanilla extract, sugar, and maple syrup, until smooth. Stir in the raspberries. Do it gently to avoid coloring the batter.

Grease a baking dish or spray it with cooking spray. Drop the batter onto the dish. Just make sure to leave some space between the pancakes. If there is some batter left, repeat the process. Cook for 10 minutes.

Herby Mushrooms with Vermouth

Prep + Cook Time: 20 minutes | Serves: 3

Ingredients

2 pounds portobello mushrooms, sliced
2 tbsp vermouth
½ tsp garlic powder

1 tbsp olive oil
2 tsp herbs
1 tbsp duck fat

Directions

Add duck fat, garlic powder and herbs in a blender, and process. Pour the mixture over the mushrooms and cover with vermouth. Place the mushrooms in the basket and cook for 10 minutes on Bake function at 350 F. Top with more vermouth and cook for 5 more minutes.

Paprika Baked Eggs

Prep + Cook Time: 10 minutes | Serves: 6

Ingredients

6 large eggs

1 tsp paprika

Directions

Preheat your Breville fryer to 300 F. Lay the eggs in the Air Fryer basket and bake for 8 minutes on Bake function. Using tongs, place the eggs in a bowl with icy water. Dip in cold water for 5 minutes before cracking the shell. Sprinkle with paprika to serve.

White Chocolate & Vanilla Brownies with Walnuts

Prep + Cook Time: 35 minutes | Serves: 6

Ingredients

6 oz dark chocolate
6 oz butter
¾ cup white sugar
3 eggs
2 tsp vanilla extract

¾ cup flour
¼ cup cocoa powder
1 cup chopped walnuts
1 cup white chocolate chips

Directions

Line a baking pan with baking paper. In a saucepan, melt chocolate and butter over low heat. Do not stop stirring until you obtain a smooth mixture. Let cool slightly, whisk in eggs and vanilla. Sift flour and cocoa and stir to mix well.

Sprinkle the walnuts over and add the white chocolate into the batter. Pour the batter into the pan and cook for 20 minutes in the Breville oven at 340 F on Bake function.

Cheddar Omelet with Soy Sauce

Prep + Cook Time: 15 minutes | Serves: 1

Ingredients

2 eggs
2 tbsp grated cheddar cheese
1 tsp soy sauce

½ onion, sliced
¼ tsp pepper
1 tbsp olive oil

Directions

Whisk the eggs along with the pepper and soy sauce. Preheat Breville on Bake function to 350 degrees F. Heat the olive oil and add the egg mixture and the onion. Cook for 8-10 minutes. Top with the grated cheddar cheese.

Amazing Apple & Brie Sandwich

Prep + Cook Time: 8 - 10 minutes | Serves: 1

Ingredients

2 bread slices
½ apple, thinly sliced

2 tsp butter
2 oz brie cheese, thinly sliced

Directions

Spread butter on the outside of the bread slices. Arrange apple slices on the inside of one bread slice. Place brie slices on top of the apple. Top with the other slice of bread. Cook in the toaster oven for 5 minutes at 350 F on Bake function. Cut diagonally and serve.

Egg & Bacon Wraps with Salsa

Prep + Cook Time: 15 minutes | Serves: 3

Ingredients

3 tortillas
2 previously scrambled eggs
3 slices bacon, cut into strips

3 tbsp salsa
3 tbsp cream cheese, divided
1 cup grated pepper Jack cheese

Directions

Preheat Breville on AirFry function to 390 F. Spread one tbsp. of cream cheese onto each tortilla. Divide the eggs and bacon between the tortillas evenly. Top with salsa. Sprinkle some grated cheese over. Roll up the tortillas. Cook for 10 minutes.

Creamy Potato Gratin with Nutmeg

Prep + Cook Time: 45 minutes | Serves: 6

INGREDIENTS

5 large potatoes
½ cup sour cream
½ cup grated cheese
½ cup milk

½ tsp nutmeg
½ tsp black pepper
½ tsp salt

DIRECTIONS

Preheat Breville on AirFry function to 390 F, peel and slice the potatoes. In a bowl, combine the sour cream, milk, pepper, salt and nutmeg. Place the potato slices in the bowl with the milk mixture and stir to coat them well.

Transfer the whole mixture to a baking dish. Cook for 25 minutes on Bake function, then sprinkle grated cheese on top and cook for 10 more minutes.

Crispy Cauliflowers with Alfredo Sauce

Prep + Cook Time: 20 minutes | Serves: 4

INGREDIENTS

4 cups cauliflower florets
1 tbsp butter, melted
¼ cup alfredo sauce

1 cup breadcrumbs
1 tsp salt

DIRECTIONS

Whisk alfredo sauce with butter. In a bowl, combine breadcrumbs with salt. Dip cauliflower into the alfredo mixture, and then coat in the crumbs. Drop the prepared florets into the Air Fryer basket. Set the temperature to 350 F and cook for 15 minutes on AirFry. Shake once.

American Cheese Sandwich

Prep + Cook Time: 10 minutes | Serves: 1

Ingredients

2 tbsp butter
2 slices bread

3 slices American cheese

Directions

Preheat Breville on Bake function to 370 degrees F. Spread one tsp of butter on the outside of each of the bread slices. Place the cheese on the inside of one bread slice. Top with the other slice. Cook in the toaster oven for 4 minutes. Flip the sandwich over and cook for an additional 4 minutes. Serve cut diagonally.

Feta & Tomato Tart with Olives

Prep + Cook Time: 40 minutes | Serves: 2

Ingredients

4 eggs
½ cup chopped tomatoes
1 cup crumbled feta cheese
1 tbsp chopped basil
1 tbsp chopped oregano

¼ cup chopped kalamata olives
¼ cup chopped onion
2 tbsp olive oil
½ cup milk
Salt and black pepper to taste

Directions

Preheat Breville on Bake function to 340 degrees F. Brush a pie pan with olive oil. Beat the eggs along with the milk and some salt and pepper. Stir in all of the remaining ingredients. Pour the egg mixture into the pan. Cook for 30 minutes.

Cinnamon & Vanilla Toast

Prep + Cook Time: 10 minutes | Serves: 6

Ingredients

12 slices bread
½ cup sugar
1 ½ tsp cinnamon

1 stick of butter, softened
1 tsp vanilla extract

Directions

Preheat Breville on Toast function to 300 F. Combine all ingredients, except the bread, in a bowl. Spread the buttery cinnamon mixture onto the bread slices. Place the bread slices in the toaster oven. Cook for 8 minutes.

Cheddar Eggs with Potatoes Frittes

Prep + Cook Time: 24 minutes | Serves: 3

INGREDIENTS

3 potatoes, thinly sliced
2 eggs, beaten
2 oz cheddar cheese

1 tbsp all-purpose flour
100 ml coconut cream

DIRECTIONS

Remove the skin of potatoes and place them in the Breville Air Fryer basket; cook for 12 minutes at 350°F on AirFry function.

To prepare the sauce, mix the two beaten eggs, coconut cream and flour until the cream mixture thickens. Remove the potatoes from the fryer, line them in the ramekin and top with the cream mixture and the cheese. Cover and cook for 12 more minutes.

Califlower Tater Tots with Cheddar

Prep + Cook Time: 35 minutes | Serves: 10

INGREDIENTS

2 lb. cauliflower florets, steamed
5 oz cheddar cheese
1 onion, diced
1 cup breadcrumbs
1 egg, beaten

1 tsp chopped parsley
1 tsp chopped oregano
1 tsp chopped chives
1 tsp garlic powder
Salt and black pepper to taste

DIRECTIONS

Mash the cauliflower and place it in a large bowl. Add the onion, parsley, oregano, chives, garlic powder, some salt and pepper, and cheddar. Mix with your hands until fully combined and form 12 balls out of the mixture.

Line a baking sheet with paper. Dip half of the tater tots into the egg and then coat with breadcrumbs. Arrange them on the baking sheet and cook in the fryer at 350 minutes for 15 minutes on AirFry function. Cook in batches.

Amazing Strawberries Pancake

Prep + Cook Time: 30 minutes | Serves: 4

Ingredients

3 eggs, beaten
2 tbsp unsalted butter
½ cup flour

2 tbsp sugar, powdered
½ cup milk
1 ½ cups fresh strawberries, sliced

Directions

Preheat Breville on AirFry function to 330 degrees F on Bake function. Add butter to a pan and melt over low heat. In a bowl, mix flour, milk, eggs and vanilla until fully incorporated. Add the mixture to the pan with melted butter.

Place the pan in your toaster oven and cook for 12-16 minutes until the pancake is fluffy and golden brown. Drizzle powdered sugar and toss sliced strawberries on top.

Caprese Sourdough Sandwich

Prep + Cook Time: 25 minutes | Serves: 2

Ingredients

4 slices sourdough bread
2 tbsp mayonnaise
2 slices ham
2 lettuce leaves

1 tomato, sliced
2 slices mozzarella cheese
Salt and black pepper to taste

Directions

On a clean board, lay the sourdough slices and spread with mayonnaise. Top 2 of the slices with ham, lettuce, tomato and mozzarella. Season with salt and pepper.

Top with the remaining two slices to form two sandwiches. Spray with oil and transfer to the Breville Air Fryer basket. Cook for 14 minutes at 340 F on Bake function, flipping once halfway through cooking. Serve hot.

Vanilla & Mango Bread with Cinnamon

Prep + Cook Time: 60 minutes | Serves: 8

Ingredients

½ cup melted butter
1 egg, lightly beaten
½ cup brown sugar
1 tsp vanilla extract
3 ripe mango, mashed

1 ½ cups plain flour
1 tsp baking powder
½ tsp grated nutmeg
½ tsp ground cinnamon

Directions

Spray the Breville baking pan with cooking spray and line with baking paper. In a bowl, whisk butter, egg, sugar, vanilla and mango. Sift in flour, baking powder, nutmeg and cinnamon and stir without overmixing.

Pour the batter into the pan and place it the toaster oven. Cook for 35 minutes at 300 F on Bake function. Make sure to check at the 20-25-minute mark. When ready, let cool before slicing it.

Meatlover Omelet with Mozzarella

Prep + Cook Time: 20 minutes | Serves: 2

Ingredients

1 beef sausage, chopped
4 slices prosciutto, chopped
3 oz salami, chopped
1 cup grated mozzarella cheese

4 eggs
1 tbsp chopped onion
1 tbsp ketchup

Directions

Preheat Breville on Bake function to 350 degrees F. Whisk the eggs with the ketchup, in a bowl. Stir in the onion. Brown the sausage in the toaster oven for 2 minutes. Meanwhile, combine the egg mixture, mozzarella cheese, salami and prosciutto. Pour the egg mixture over the sausage and give it a stir. Cook for 10 minutes.

Almond & Berry Oat Bars

Prep + Cook Time: 40 minutes | Serves: 10

Ingredients

3 cups rolled oats
½ cup ground almonds
½ cup flour
1 tsp baking powder
1 tsp ground cinnamon

3 eggs, lightly beaten
½ cup canola oil
⅓ cup milk
2 tsp vanilla extract
2 cups mixed berries

Directions

Spray the Breville baking pan with cooking spray. In a bowl, add oats, almonds, flour, baking powder and cinnamon into and stir well. In another bowl, whisk eggs, oil, milk, and vanilla.

Stir the wet ingredients gently into the oat mixture. Fold in the berries. Pour the mixture in the pan and place in the toaster oven. Cook for 30 minutes at 330 F on Bake function. When ready, check if the bars are nice and soft.

Ham Shirred Eggs with Parmesan

Prep + Cook Time: 20 minutes | Serves: 2

Ingredients

2 tsp butter, for greasing
4 eggs, divided
2 tbsp heavy cream
4 slices of ham
3 tbsp Parmesan cheese

¼ tsp paprika
¾ tsp salt
¼ tsp pepper
2 tsp chopped chives

Directions

Preheat Breville on AirFry function to 320 F. Grease a pie pan with the butter. Arrange the ham slices on the bottom of the pan to cover it completely. Whisk one egg along with the heavy cream, salt and pepper, in a bowl.

Pour the mixture over the ham slices. Crack the other eggs over the ham. Sprinkle with Parmesan cheese. Cook for 14 minutes. Season with paprika, garnish with chives and serve with bread.

Feta & Spinach Omelet with Mushrooms

Prep + Cook Time: 10 minutes | Serves: 2

Ingredients

4 eggs, lightly beaten
2 tbsp heavy cream
2 cups spinach, chopped
1 cup chopped mushrooms

3 oz feta cheese, crumbled
A handful of fresh parsley, chopped
Salt and black pepper

Directions

Spray your Breville Air Fryer basket with cooking spray. In a bowl, whisk eggs and until combined. Stir in spinach, mushrooms, feta, parsley, salt and pepper.

Pour into the basket and cook in your Breville for 6 minutes at 350 F on Bake function. Serve with a touch of tangy tomato relish.

Onion Tart with Feta

Prep + Cook Time: 30 minutes | Serves: 3

Ingredients

3½ pounds Feta cheese
Black pepper to taste
1 whole onion, chopped
2 tbsp parsley, chopped

1 egg yolk
Olive oil for drizzling
5 sheets frozen filo pastry

Directions

Cut each of the 5 filo sheets into three equal-sized strips. Cover the strips with oil. In a bowl, mix onion, pepper, feta, salt, egg yolk, and parsley.

Make triangles using the cut strips and add a little bit of the feta mixture on top of each triangle. Place the triangles in the basket and cook for 5 minutes at 400 F on Bake function. Serve, drizzled with oil and green onions.

Thyme Cheddar Hash Browns

Prep + Cook Time: 25 minutes | Serves: 4

Ingredients

4 russet potatoes, peeled, grated
1 brown onion, chopped
3 garlic cloves, chopped
½ cup grated cheddar cheese

1 egg, lightly beaten
Salt and black pepper
3 tbsp finely thyme sprigs

Directions

In a bowl, mix with hands potatoes, onion, garlic, cheese, egg, salt, black pepper and thyme. Spray the fryer with cooking spray.

Press the hash brown mixture into the basket and cook for 9 minutes at 400 F on Bake function, shaking once halfway through cooking. When ready, ensure the hash browns are golden and crispy.

Balsamic Chicken with Spinach & Kale

Prep + Cook Time: 20 minutes | Serves: 1

Ingredients

½ cup baby spinach leaves
½ cup shredded romaine
3 large kale leaves, chopped
4 oz chicken breasts, cut into cubes

3 tbsp olive oil, divided
1 tsp balsamic vinegar
1 garlic clove, minced
Salt and black pepper to taste

Directions

Place the chicken, 1 tbsp. olive oil and garlic, in a bowl. Season with salt and pepper and toss to combine.

Put on a lined baking dish and cook for 14 minutes at 390F on Broil function. Meanwhile, place the greens in a large bowl. Add the remaining olive oil and balsamic vinegar. Season with salt and pepper and toss to combine. Top with the chicken.

Feta & Chorizo Corn Frittata

Prep + Cook Time: 12 minutes | Serves: 2

Ingredients

3 eggs
1 large potato, boiled and cubed
½ cup frozen corn
½ cup feta cheese, crumbled

1 tbsp chopped parsley
½ chorizo, sliced
1 tbsp olive oil
Salt and black pepper to taste

Directions

Preheat Breville on AirFry function to 330 F. Brush the chorizo with olive oil and cook it in the toaster oven for 3 minutes. Beat the eggs with some salt and pepper in a bowl. Stir in all of the remaining ingredients. Pour the mixture into the baking pan of Breville oven, give it a good stir, and cook for 8 minutes on Bake function.

Quick Cheddar Omelet

Prep + Cook Time: 15 minutes | Serves: 1

Ingredients

2 eggs, beaten
Black pepper to taste
1 cup cheddar cheese, shredded

1 whole onion, chopped
2 tbsp soy sauce

Directions

Preheat Breville on AirFry function to 340 F. Drizzle soy sauce over the chopped onions. Place the onions in the Air Fryer basket and cook for 8 minutes on Bake function. In a bowl, mix the beaten eggs with salt and pepper.

Pour the egg mixture over onions (in the cooking basket) and cook for 3 minutes. Add cheddar cheese over eggs and bake for 2 more minutes. Serve and enjoy!

Basil Parmesan Bagel

Prep + Cook Time: 6 minutes | Serves: 1

Ingredients

2 tbsp butter, softened
1 tsp dried basil
1 tsp dried parsley
1 tsp garlic powder

1 tbsp Parmesan cheese
Salt and black pepper to taste
1 bagel

Directions

Preheat Breville on Bake function to 370 degrees. Cut the bagel in half. Place in the fryer and cook for 3 minutes. Combine the butter, Parmesan, garlic, basil, and parsley in a small bowl. Season with salt and pepper, to taste.

Spread the mixture onto the toasted bagel. Return the bagel to the fryer and cook for 3 more minutes.

Basil Cottage Omelet with Kale

Prep + Cook Time: 15 minutes | Serves: 1

Ingredients

3 eggs
3 tbsp cottage cheese
3 tbsp chopped kale
½ tbsp chopped basil

½ tbsp chopped parsley
Salt and black pepper to taste
1 tsp olive oil

Directions+

Beat the eggs with salt and pepper, in a bowl. Stir in the rest of the ingredients. Drizzle the baking pan with olive oil. Pour the mixture into the Breville oven and cook for 10 minutes on Bake function at 360 F, until slightly golden and set.

Italian Sandwich

Prep + Cook Time: 7 minutes | Serves: 1

Ingredients

2 slices of bread
4 tomato slices
4 mozzarella slices

1 tbsp olive oil
1 tbsp chopped basil
Salt and black pepper to taste

Directions

Preheat Breville on Toast function to 350 degrees F. Place the bread slices in the toaster oven and toast for 5 minutes. Arrange two tomato slices on each bread slice. Season with salt and pepper.

Top each slice with 2 mozzarella slices. Return to the oven and cook for 1 minute more. Drizzle the caprese toasts with olive oil and top with chopped basil.

Buttery Orange Toast

Prep + Cook Time: 15 minutes | Serves: 6

Ingredients

12 slices bread
½ cup sugar
1 stick butter

1½ tbsp vanilla extract
1½ tbsp cinnamon
2 oranges, zested

Directions

Mix butter, sugar, and vanilla extract and microwave the mixture for 30 seconds until melts. Add in orange zest. Pour the mixture over bread slices. Lay the bread slices in Breville Air Fryer basket and cook for 5 minutes at 400 F on Toast function. Serve with banana and berry sauce.

Honey Berry Pastry

Prep + Cook Time: 20 minutes | Serves: 3

Ingredients

3 pastry dough sheets
2 tbsp mashed strawberries
2 tbsp mashed raspberries

¼ tsp vanilla extract
2 cups cream cheese
1 tbsp honey

Directions

Preheat fryer on Bake function to 375 F. Divide cream cheese between the dough sheets. In a bowl, combine berries, honey and vanilla. Divide the mixture between the pastry sheets. Pinch the ends of the sheets, to form puff. Place in the toaster oven and cook for 15 minutes.

Tortilla de Patatas with Spinach

Prep + Cook Time: 35 minutes | Serves: 4

Ingredients

3 cups potato cubes, boiled
2 cups spinach, chopped
5 eggs, lightly beaten
¼ cup heavy cream

1 cup grated mozzarella cheese
½ cup parsley, chopped
Fresh thyme, chopped
Salt and black pepper to taste

Directions

Spray the Breville Air Fryer basket with oil. Arrange the potatoes inside. In a bowl, whisk eggs, cream, spinach, mozzarella, parsley, thyme, salt and pepper, and pour over the potatoes. Cook in your Breville for 16 minutes at 400 F on Bake function, until nice and golden.

Easy Parsnip Hash Browns

Prep + Cook Time: 20 minutes | Serves: 2

Ingredients

1 large parsnip, grated
3 eggs, beaten
½ tsp garlic powder
¼ tsp nutmeg

1 tbsp olive oil
1 cup flour
Salt and black pepper to taste

Directions

In a bowl, combine flour, eggs, parsnip, nutmeg, and garlic powder. Season with salt and pepper. Form patties out of the mixture. Drizzle the basket with olive oil and arrange the patties inside. Cook for 15 minutes on AirFry function at 360 F. Serve with garlic mayo.

Peanut Butter & Honey Porridge

Prep + Cook Time: 5 minutes | Serves: 4

Ingredients

2 cups steel-cut oats
1 cup flax seeds
1 tbsp peanut butter

1 tbsp butter
4 cups milk
4 tbsp honey

Directions

Preheat Breville on Bake function to 390 degrees F. Combine all of the ingredients in an ovenproof bowl. Place in the toaster oven and cook for 7 minutes. Stir and serve.

Egg English Muffin with Bacon

Prep + Cook Time: 10 minutes | Serves: 1

Ingredients

1 egg
1 English muffin

2 slices of bacon
Salt and black pepper to taste

Directions

Preheat Breville on Bake function to 395 F. Crack the egg into a ramekin. Place the muffin, egg and bacon in the toaster oven. Cook for 9 minutes. Let cool slightly so you can assemble the sandwich.

Cut the muffin in half. Place the egg on one half and season with salt and pepper. Arrange the bacon on top. Top with the other muffin half.

Parsley Sausage Patties

Prep + Cook Time: 20 minutes | Serves: 4

Ingredients

1 lb ground Italian sausage
¼ cup breadcrumbs
1 tsp dried parsley
1 tsp red pepper flakes

½ tsp salt
¼ tsp black pepper
¼ tsp garlic powder
1 egg, beaten

Directions

Preheat Breville on Bake function to 350 degrees F. Combine all of the ingredients in a large bowl. Line a baking sheet with parchment paper.

Make patties out of the sausage mixture and arrange them on the baking sheet. Cook for 15 minutes, flipping once halfway through cooking.

Quick Mac & Cheese

Prep + Cook Time: 15 minutes | Serves: 2

Ingredients

1 cup cooked macaroni
1 cup grated cheddar cheese
½ cup warm milk

1 tbsp Parmesan cheese
Salt and black pepper to taste

Directions

Preheat Breville on AirFry function to 350 degrees F. Add the macaroni to an ovenproof baking dish. Stir in the cheddar and milk. Season with salt and pepper, to taste. Place the dish in the toaster oven and cook for 10 minutes. Sprinkle with Parmesan cheese, to serve.

Basil Prosciutto Costini with Mozzarella

Prep + Cook Time: 7 minutes | Serves: 1

Ingredients

½ cup finely chopped tomatoes
3 oz chopped mozzarella
3 prosciutto slices, chopped

1 tbsp olive oil
1 tsp dried basil
6 small slices of French bread

Directions

Preheat Breville on Toast function to 350 degrees F. Place the bread slices in the toaster oven and toast for 5 minutes. Top the bread with tomatoes, prosciutto and mozzarella. Sprinkle the basil over the mozzarella. Drizzle with olive oil. Return to oven and cook for 1 more minute, enough to become melty and warm.

Easy French-Style Apple Cake

Prep + Cook Time: 25 minutes | Serves: 9

Ingredients

2 ¾ oz flour
5 tbsp sugar
1 ¼ oz butter

3 tbsp cinnamon
2 whole apple, sliced

Directions

Preheat Breville on Bake function to 360 F and in a bowl, mix 3 tbsp sugar, butter and flour; form pastry using the batter. Roll out the pastry on a floured surface and transfer it to the fryer's basket. Arrange the apple slices atop.

Cover apples with sugar and cinnamon; cook for 20 minutes. Sprinkle with powdered sugar and mint to serve.

DESSERTS

Orange Sponge Cake

Prep + Cook Time: 50 minutes | Serves: 6

Ingredients

9 oz sugar

9 oz self-rising flour

9 oz butter

3 eggs

1 tsp baking powder

1 tsp vanilla extract

zest of 1 orange

Frosting:

4 egg whites

Juice of 1 orange

1 tsp orange food coloring

zest of 1 orange

7 oz superfine sugar

Directions

Preheat Breville on Bake function to 160 F and place all cake ingredients, in a bowl and beat with an electric mixer. Transfer half of the batter into a prepared cake pan; bake for 15 minutes. Repeat the process for the other half of the batter.

Meanwhile, prepare the frosting by beating all frosting ingredients together. Spread the frosting mixture on top of one cake. Top with the other cake.

Apricot Crumble with Blackberries

Prep + Cook Time: 30 minutes | Serves: 4

Ingredients

2 ½ cups fresh apricots, de-stoned and cubed

1 cup fresh blackberries

½ cup sugar

2 tbsp lemon Juice

1 cup flour

Salt as needed

5 tbsp butter

Directions

Add the apricot cubes to a bowl and mix with lemon juice, 2 tbsp sugar, and blackberries. Scoop the mixture into a greased dish and spread it evenly. In another bowl, mix flour and remaining sugar.

Add 1 tbsp of cold water and butter and keep mixing until you have a crumbly mixture. Preheat Breville on Bake function to 390 F and place the fruit mixture in the basket. Top with crumb mixture and cook for 20 minutes.

Apple & Cinnamon Pie

Prep + Cook Time: 30 minutes | Serves: 9

Ingredients

4 apples, diced
2 oz butter, melted
2 oz sugar
1 oz brown sugar

2 tsp cinnamon
1 egg, beaten
3 large puff pastry sheets
¼ tsp salt

Directions

Whisk white sugar, brown sugar, cinnamon, salt, and butter, together. Place the apples in a baking dish and coat them with the mixture. Place the baking dish in the toaster oven, and cook for 10 minutes at 350 F on Bake function.

Meanwhile, roll out the pastry on a floured flat surface, and cut each sheet into 6 equal pieces. Divide the apple filling between the pieces. Brush the edges of the pastry squares with the egg.

Fold them and seal the edges with a fork. Place on a lined baking sheet and cook in the fryer at 350 F for 8 minutes. Flip over, increase the temperature to 390 F, and cook for 2 more minutes.

Berry Crumble with Lemon

Prep + Cook Time: 30 minutes | Serves: 6

Ingredients

12 oz fresh strawberries
7 oz fresh raspberries
5 oz fresh blueberries
5 tbsp cold butter
2 tbsp lemon juice

1 cup flour
½ cup sugar
1 tbsp water
A pinch of salt

Directions

Gently mass the berries, but make sure there are chunks left. Mix with the lemon juice and 2 tbsp. of the sugar.

Place the berry mixture at the bottom of a prepared round cake. Combine the flour with the salt and sugar, in a bowl. Add the water and rub the butter with your fingers until the mixture becomes crumbled.

Arrange the crisp batter over the berries. Cook in the fryer at 390 F for 20 minutes on Bake function. Serve chilled.

Vanilla-Lemon Cupcakes with Lemon Glaze

Prep + Cook Time: 30 minutes | Serves: 6

Ingredients

1 cup flour
½ cup sugar
1 small egg
1 tsp lemon zest
¾ tsp baking powder

¼ tsp baking soda
½ tsp salt
2 tbsp vegetable oil
½ cup milk
½ tsp vanilla extract

Glaze:

½ cup powdered sugar

2 tsp lemon juice

Directions

Preheat Breville on Bake function to 350 F, and combine all dry muffin ingredients, in a bowl. In another bowl, whisk together the wet ingredients. Gently combine the two mixtures. Divide the batter between 6 greased muffin tins. Place the muffin tins in the toaster oven and cook for 13 to 16 minutes.

Meanwhile, whisk the powdered sugar with the lemon juice. Spread the glaze over the muffins.

Handmade Donuts

Prep + Cook Time: 25 minutes | Serves: 4

Ingredients

8 oz self-rising flour
1 tsp baking powder
½ cup milk

2 ½ tbsp butter
1 egg
2 oz brown sugar

Directions

Preheat Breville on Bake function to 350 F, and beat the butter with the sugar, until smooth. Beat in eggs, and milk. In a bowl, combine the flour with the baking powder. Gently fold the flour into the butter mixture.

Form donut shapes and cut off the center with cookie cutters. Arrange on a lined baking sheet and cook in the fryer for 15 minutes. Serve with whipped cream or icing.

Apple Treat with Raisins

Prep + Cook Time: 15 minutes | Serves: 4

Ingredients

4 apples, cored
1 ½ oz almonds

¾ oz raisins
2 tbsp sugar

Directions

Preheat Breville on Bake function to 360 F and in a bowl, mix sugar, almonds, raisins. Blend the mixture using a hand mixer. Fill cored apples with the almond mixture. Place the prepared apples in your Air fryer basket and cook for 10 minutes. Serve with powdered sugar.

Almond Cookies with Dark Chocolate

Prep + Cook Time: 145 minutes | Serves: 4

Ingredients

8 egg whites
½ tsp almond extract
1 ⅓ cups sugar
¼ tsp salt

2 tsp lemon juice
1 ½ tsp vanilla extract
Melted dark chocolate to drizzle

Directions

In a mixing bowl, add egg whites, salt, and lemon juice. Beat using an electric mixer until foamy. Slowly add the sugar and continue beating until completely combined; add the almond and vanilla extracts. Beat until stiff peaks form and glossy.

Line a round baking sheet with parchment paper. Fill a piping bag with the meringue mixture and pipe as many mounds on the baking sheet as you can leaving 2-inch spaces between each mound.

Place the baking sheet in the fryer basket and bake at 250 F for 5 minutes on Bake function. Reduce the temperature to 220 F and bake for 15 more minutes. Then, reduce the temperature to 190 F and cook for 15 minutes. Remove the baking sheet and let the meringues cool for 2 hours. Drizzle with dark chocolate and serve.

Air Fried Banana with Sesame Seeds

Prep + Cook Time: 15 minutes | Serves: 5

Ingredients

1 ½ cups flour
5 bananas, sliced
1 tsp salt
3 tbsp sesame seeds

1 cup water
2 eggs, beaten
1 tsp baking powder
½ tbsp sugar

Directions

Preheat Breville on Bake function to 340 F.

In a bowl, mix salt, sesame seeds, flour, baking powder, eggs, sugar, and water. Coat sliced bananas with the flour mixture; place the prepared slices in the Air Fryer basket; cook for 8-10 minutes. Serve chilled.

Vanilla Brownies with Chocolate Chips

Prep + Cook Time: 25 minutes | Serves: 2

Ingredients

1 whole egg, beaten
¼ cup chocolate chips
2 tbsp white sugar
⅓ cup flour

2 tbsp safflower oil
1 tsp vanilla
¼ cup cocoa powder

Directions

Preheat Breville on Bake function to 320 F and in a bowl, mix the beaten egg, sugar, oil, and vanilla. In another bowl, mix cocoa powder and flour. Add the flour mixture to the vanilla mixture and stir until fully incorporated. Pour the mixture into the Breville baking pan abjnd sprinkle chocolate chips on top. Cook for 20 minutes. Chill and cut into squares to serve.

Cinnamon & Honey Apples with Hazelnuts

Prep + Cook Time: 13 minutes | Serves: 2

Ingredients

4 apples
1 oz butter
2 oz breadcrumbs
Zest of 1 orange

2 tbsp chopped hazelnuts
2 oz mixed seeds
1 tsp cinnamon
2 tbsp honey

Directions

Preheat Breville on Bake function to 350 F and core the apples. Make sure to also score their skin to prevent from splitting. Combine the remaining ingredients in a bowl; stuff the apples with the mixture and cook for 10 minutes. Serve topped with chopped hazelnuts.

Pan-Fried Bananas

Prep + Cook Time: 15 minutes | Serves: 8

Ingredients

8 bananas
3 tbsp vegetable oil
3 tbsp corn flour

1 egg white
¾ cup breadcrumbs

Directions

Preheat Breville on Toast function to 350 F. Combine oil and breadcrumbs in a bowl. Coat the bananas with the corn flour, brush with egg white, and dip in the breadcrumb mixture. Arrange on a lined baking sheet and cook for 8-12 minutes.

Delicious Banana Pastry with Berries

Prep + Cook Time: 15 minutes | Serves: 2

Ingredients

3 bananas, sliced

3 tbsp honey

2 puff pastry sheets, cut into thin strips

Fresh berries to serve

Directions

Preheat Breville on AirFry function to 340 F and place the banana slices into the cooking basket. Cover with the pastry strips and top with honey. Cook for 10-12 minutes on Bake function. Serve with fresh berries.

Easy Mocha Cake

Prep + Cook Time: 30 minutes | Serves: 2

Ingredients

¼ cup butter

½ tsp instant coffee

1 tbsp black coffee, brewed

1 egg

¼ cup sugar

¼ cup flour

1 tsp cocoa powder

A pinch of salt

Powdered sugar, for icing

Directions

Preheat Breville on Bake function to 330 F and grease a small ring cake pan. Beat the sugar and egg together in a bowl. Beat in cocoa, instant and black coffees; stir in salt and flour. Transfer the batter to the prepared pan. Cook for 15 minutes. Dust with powdered sugar and serve.

Choco Lava Cakes

Prep + Cook Time: 20 minutes | Serves: 4

Ingredients

3 ½ oz butter, melted

3 ½ tbsp sugar

1 ½ tbsp self-rising flour

3 ½ oz dark chocolate, melted

2 eggs

Directions

Grease 4 ramekins with butter. Preheat Breville on Bake function to 375 F. Beat eggs and sugar until frothy. Stir in butter and chocolate; gently fold in the flour.

Divide the mixture between the ramekins and bake in the fryer for 10 minutes. Let cool for 2 minutes before turning the cakes upside down onto serving plates.

Mouthwatering Chocolate Soufflé

Prep + Cook Time: 25 minutes | Serves: 2

Ingredients

2 eggs, whites and yolks separated
¼ cup butter, melted
2 tbsp flour

3 tbsp sugar
3 oz chocolate, melted
½ tsp vanilla extract

Directions

Beat the yolks along with the sugar and vanilla extract; stir in butter, chocolate, and flour. Preheat Breville on Bake function to 330 F and whisk the whites until a stiff peak forms. Working in batches, gently combine the egg whites with the chocolate mixture. Divide the batter between two greased ramekins. Cook for 14-18 minutes.

Maple Pecan Pie

Prep + Cook Time: 1 hr 10 minutes | Serves: 4

Ingredients

¾ cup maple syrup
2 eggs
½ tsp salt
¼ tsp nutmeg
½ tsp cinnamon
2 tbsp almond butter

2 tbsp brown sugar
½ cup chopped pecans
1 tbsp butter, melted
1 8-inch pie dough
¾ tsp vanilla extract

Directions

Preheat Breville on Toast function to 350 F, and coat the pecans with the melted butter. Place the pecans in the fryer and toast them for 5 minutes. Place the pie crust into the baking pan, and scatter the pecans over.

Whisk together all remaining ingredients in a bowl. Pour the maple mixture over the pecans. Set Breville to 320 F and cook the pie for 25 minutes on Bake function.

Made in the USA
Middletown, DE
12 January 2020